PRESIDENTIAL RESIDENCES IN FRANCE

EXECUTIVE EDITOR
Suzanne Tise-Isoré
Style & Design Collection

EDITORIAL ADVISER
Karine Huguenaud

EDITORIAL COORDINATION
Lara Lo Calzo

GRAPHIC DESIGN
Bernard Lagacé

TRANSLATION FROM THE FRENCH
Deke Dusinberre

COPY EDITING AND PROOFREADING
Lindsay Porter

PRODUCTION
Élodie Conjat

COLOR SEPARATION
Les Artisans du Regard, Paris

Printed in Barcelona (Spain) by Indice

Simultaneously published in French
as *Résidences présidentielles*

Flammarion S.A.
87, quai Panhard-et-Levassor
75647 Paris cedex 13
editions.flammarion.com
styleetdesign-flammarion.com

21 22 23 3 2 1
ISBN: 978-2-08-024753-7
Legal Deposit: 09/2021

FRONT COVER The Golden Room in the Élysée Palace now serves as the office of the French president. Centrally placed on the second floor of the residence, the room was decorated by architect Joseph Eugène Lacroix in 1858–61, and has now been restored to its original decoration. It overlooks the garden and was initially designed to host parties—nothing predisposed it to become the center of French government.
BACK COVER, TOP At the Élysée Palace, the Silver Room (left) and the Ballroom (right).
BOTTOM The Pavilion of La Lanterne in Versailles, the stag-head gate (left) and the Fort of Brégançon in Bormes-les-Mimosas (right).
ENDPAPERS Detail of the scrolling foliage that decorates the Golden Room. The woodwork was painted "in color against a gold ground" by Jean-Louis Godon in 1861. He adopted an eighteenth-century-revival style that reflected the Second Empire's eclectic taste, which thrived in this residence once inhabited by Madame de Pompadour.

PRESIDENTIAL RESIDENCES IN FRANCE

Text Adrien Goetz, Institut de France Photography Ambroise Tézenas

Flammarion

CONTENTS

FACING PAGE A gateway on Avenue Gabriel, providing a back entrance via the palace grounds, is crowned by symbols of the Republic of France—the monogram RF and the Gallic rooster. The latter emblem, punning on the Latin word *gallus* for "Gaul" and "rooster," is the democratic successor to France's imperial eagle.

ANNO
1900

FOREWORD

This is the first book to reveal the recent restoration and current furnishing of France's presidential residence, the Élysée Palace, as well as to introduce readers to other little-known sites of presidential power such as the Marigny mansion in Paris, the pavilion in Versailles called La Lanterne, and the Fort of Brégançon on the Riviera. With the help of France's National Furniture Depository, all these residences have been redecorated in a new spirit.

From reception rooms to grand dinners to gardens and even behind the scenes, these pages trace the French tradition of merging fine arts with decorative crafts, a tradition that each president attempts to reinterpret and reinvigorate.

Thanks to historic pictures and recent photographs, the silent language of interior decoration here tells the tale of a complex, evolving organism. For despite the cliché of France's "gilded palaces," these residences function as subtle machines of government, hosting small meetings as well as major press conferences, allowing for withdrawal and reflection as well as carefully staged events employing the subtle, coded art of public relations.

Restoration doesn't mean seeking to recreate a legendary "original" state—which is gone forever—but rather to restore meaning and movement, to imbue a forgotten, historic spirit with new significance, to invent modern usages and new forms of protocol.

The full history of these residences, none of which was designed to serve as a palace, is revealed here, starting with the likes of the Count of Évreux and Madame de Pompadour, who imparted soul to the Élysée. Yet although key historical figures occupy the foreground, the real protagonists of this story are the meticulous, scrupulous artisans in the background, who make the wheels turn but who vanish whenever a photographer shows up. This is not an anecdotal history of the Élysée and its "occupants," as so often recounted, but rather an exploration of sites of collective memory that reflect all the richness of France.

Adrien Goetz, Institut de France

FACING PAGE Athena olive branches symbolically intertwine with the laurels of victory on the woodwork of the doors of the Library.

HOME TO FRENCH PRESIDENTS

In France, every presidential election presents itself as a big bang, as the start of a new era whose impact may range from modest "change with continuity" to a total "transition from darkness to light." The successive redecorations of the Élysée Palace and other presidential residences in France translate this rhetoric into furnishings, lamps, and carpets. Whereas the rhetoric about a new era never changes, the regular redecorations suggest otherwise. Architecture also plays a coded role in the protocol of change: the newly elected president accompanies his predecessor to the foot of the front steps, or sometimes a few paces further into the courtyard. No ornament is purely decorative, no room remains unexpressive for someone able to interpret it.

Residing and presiding within the same walls is no mean feat. Representation and work are two activities that call for different furnishings. A president's choice of interior is a kind of foreign policy, and is always suspected of concealing secrets, regardless of whether too much or too little is displayed. In the Élysée, secrets seem to be concocted the better to reveal them: the office of the president—which in France is viewed as the successor to the king's bedchamber at Versailles and the throne room in the Tuileries Palace—must be seen by all when thrown open to the public each year on European Heritage Day. This popular event offers everyone a glimpse of Eleusinian Mysteries. Back in the 1970s, barely had a strategic underground headquarters (the "Jupiter" bunker) been built by President Valéry Giscard d'Estaing (1974–81), than cameras were invited in—with the inevitable shot of a door suddenly swinging shut to prevent deeper intrusion. The French also enjoyed following the vacations of President Georges Pompidou (1969–74) and his wife at the Fort of Brégançon, a "crooked house" worthy of Agatha Christie. And the public was allowed a two-minute peek of the cabinet office in the Élysée when President François Mitterrand (1981–95) had to host, for the first time in French history, a cabinet controlled by the opposition party. In 2020, President Emmanuel Macron (2017–present) even filmed himself with his phone in the Versailles retreat known as La Lanterne—maybe because, in the end, there was nothing "secret" about the place. Mitterrand's bright idea of opening one side of the Ballroom (used for all kinds of ceremonial events), so that it overlooked the back garden of the Élysée—another sacred realm of presidential power—was significant: he realized that the French wanted to peer through the walls. He also felt he was suffocating in that boxy room decorated in red and gold like an old-fashioned theater. A head of state requires not just carefully composed images but also occasional breaths of fresh air. The history of French presidents and presidential residences is nothing other than an imaginative construct, built up layer by layer.

Retracing the saga of these "sites of collective memory"—to borrow the concept of Pierre Nora's four-volume history, *Rethinking France,* which included Notre-Dame Cathedral, Versailles, the Napoleonic Code, and the Louvre, but *not* the Élysée Palace—means delving into archive images. There we see that change has been constant: President Sadi Carnot (1887–94) installed his office

FACING PAGE The Élysée Palace–originally called the Hôtel d'Évreux–seen from the grounds.

in what is now the Napoleon III Library, as did Armand Fallières (1906–13), but the books had to be replaced by a tapestry and the heavy Empire-style desk by an elegant eighteenth-century one designed by Charles Cressent. This, in turn, was later moved upstairs when a president who disapproved of a frivolous décor in a palace with a frivolous past transferred his office to the stately Golden Room. Cressent's writing desk became legendary, and was thought to have become immutable once it was adopted by President Charles de Gaulle (1958–69). Yet Giscard d'Estaing later abandoned the Golden Room for a corner office, where he installed the desk, made by Jean-Henri Riesener, that he had used when minister of finance. Mitterrand moved back into de Gaulle's office, which he redecorated during his second term with modern blue furniture by Pierre Paulin, the designer who had decorated several rooms for Pompidou. On his official photograph, President Macron is shown leaning against the Cressent desk—back in place—on which he immediately placed a double clock that had "always" been in the Murat Room, thereby suggesting a "clockmaker" analogy: cabinet meetings, held in the Ambassadors Room (a strangely obsolete name for the room) would henceforth run like clockwork thanks to President Macron and his prime minister, seated opposite him. Today the President, who works in a corner office upstairs, has had the Golden Room restored, using it for more official meetings and installing furniture by contemporary designers—his desk is Thierry Lemaire's Modèle K and his Passion armchair was designed by Philippe Starck (who as a young man had worked on Mitterrand's private apartments at the Élysée).

Beyond individual taste, the current state of the presidential palace—still listed in inventories by its original name of Hôtel d'Évreux—is the culmination of major renovations carried out at the rate of one large room per year. Deciphering the language of furnishings and understanding the successive functions of a given room, however, is not all that complex: the history of the Élysée, like many grand residences, is the product of changes that, if often contradictory, are always political.

The "furnished lodging," as de Gaulle wittily dubbed the Élysée, was designed to be unfurnished and refurnished, but the operation is more than an assertion of personal taste. Giscard d'Estaing set the tone right from the entrance hall where he placed Jean-Baptiste Lemoyne the Younger's sculpture *Vertumnus and Pomona* (having himself researched an engraving that showed the right height for its base), yet he also considered replacing the steam radiators dating from Fallière's day (1906–13). Under Mitterrand, Lemoyne's frivolous sculpture was sent back to the Louvre and replaced by one by Arman, *Homage to the Revolution of 1789,* an accumulation of two hundred French flags to celebrate the two hundredth anniversary of the French Revolution; this modern work was nevertheless flanked by bronze-and-crystal candle stands by Thomire and Chagot in a Bourbon-Restoration style.

The many properties formerly allocated to the French presidency have now been reduced: the Casimir-Perier estate known as the Château of Vizille, bought by the government in 1924, where presidents Albert Lebrun (1932–40) and René Coty (1954–59) spent their vacations, has become a museum of the French Revolution; the Pavillon de Marly is now a public reminder of the former château at Marly-le-Roi; the Trianon-sous-Bois wing of Versailles, equipped to receive guests of President de Gaulle and his wife, Yvonne, is now open as an historic curiosity (the restoration campaign helped to save the Grand Trianon);

FACING PAGE, TOP The residence known as La Lanterne was originally designed to house the governor of the royal estate of Versailles, but is now a retreat for the French president.

FACING PAGE, BOTTOM The Fort of Brégançon, on a rocky outcrop overlooking the Mediterranean Sea, has been associated with presidential vacations since the days of George Pompidou (1969–74), yet can also serve as a site of government.

the Château of Rambouillet is now a national monument open to the public; and the small estate of Souzy-la-Briche no longer hosts the head of state.

Thus there remain only three places of residence, each of which plays its own role. The first, the Élysée, is a private mansion become palace—itself a contradiction. Furthermore, the palace must flaunt the grandeur of France all the while handling a great deal of business—two very different tasks. It therefore has annexes: the offices of the recently restored Palais de l'Alma (which has nothing palatial about it) between the Musée du Quai Branly and the Russian Orthodox Cathedral; several houses on Rue de l'Élysée; and, on the other side of Avenue de Marigny, a large nineteenth-century building in the grand Rothschild style, magnificent but impractical. The second presidential residence is a small estate at Versailles, known as La Lanterne. The third is the Fort of Brégançon on the French Riviera—which is perhaps even more beguiling than the Élysée.

Places of reception and retreat, machines of government and maintainers of secrets, sites of ceremony, solitude, and action, these theaters of history great and small are the successors to Versailles's Hall of Mirrors—they reflect a certain history of France.

BELOW Since June 1994, the entrance hall where visitors are greeted has hosted a white marble and bronze sculpture by Arman, *Homage to the Revolution of 1789* (1984), flanked by Restoration-era candle stands by Thomire and Chagot.

FACING PAGE President Charles de Gaulle chose the Golden Room for his office in 1959. His choice was copied by all presidents except Valéry Giscard d'Estaing and now Emmanuel Macron, who works in a nearby "corner office." The Golden Room nevertheless retains its role as a formal office for receiving official visitors.

PAGES 14-15 An aerial view of the grounds of the Élysée Palace flanked by Rue du Faubourg Saint-Honoré, Avenue de Marigny, and Rue de l'Élysée. What political pundits call "the Château" is clearly part of the urban fabric.

THE ÉLYSÉE PALACE

HÔTEL D'ÉVREUX, PARIS

The Élysée is not a palace. It is a gem of a building, a private mansion never designed to reflect the pomp of state. Its name means Elysium, the Homeric, heavenly dwelling place of heroes and happy souls—yet Elysium also belongs to Hades, the world of the dead. Nothing more natural, then, to come across ghosts here. Starting in the eighteenth century, the majestic avenue known as the Champs-Élysées was slowly laid out, starting from the Tuileries Palace, more or less aligned with the Louvre, steadily advancing across the marshland. Flanking it was a thirty-acre field owned by two gardeners, Jean Le Nôtre and Jean Le Bouteux, who installed a nursery with a little house there. The place was dubbed "The Gourds" (also a slang term for "jugheads"), a name that has fortunately faded from memory. Jean's son, the famous gardener André Le Nôtre, bought the property with swift speculation in mind (Louis XIV had granted Le Nôtre a coat of arms that featured three slugs). André, who designed the gardens at Versailles and created an entirely new style, was also an art lover, the first of many whose names are associated with the birth of the Élysée Palace. The shape of the plot, the one still occupied by the presidential palace, was drawn even before a house was built on it.

In 1718 the financier John Law bought the plot on behalf of the Count of Évreux, Louis de La Tour d'Auvergne, who was the fourth son of the Duke of Bouillon (a name that Proust employed for the character of Basin de Guermantes-Bouillon, Prince of Laumes) and Marie-Anne Mancini, niece of the royal counselor, Cardinal Mazarin. More important, the count married the daughter of Antoine Crozat, whom Saint-Simon described as "the richest man in Paris" (where everyone moved once Louis XIV died, abandoning Versailles). The Crozat family were social climbers, enjoying their most unlikely triumph at the Louvre as late as 2014, when the new galleries of decorative art showcased the famous "Crozat furniture" (belonging to Antoine's brother, Pierre, the famous patron of the artist Watteau), beneath the gaze of Hyacinthe Rigaud's famous portrait of Louis XIV in coronation robes—which even Molière's bourgeois gentleman would never have imagined.

The Count of Évreux had sought the office of Master of the Royal Hunt, which the regent, the Duke of Orléans, mischievously promised to grant, in person, at the count's Paris residence, knowing he didn't have one. So the count erected one on the quick, decorating just a few reception rooms. France's current presidential residence was therefore built to meet a challenge and to impress—a typically French spirit permeated the former marshland.

PAGE 16 Seen from the grounds, the Élysée combines the features of an urban mansion with a stately country home. **PAGE 17** The courtyard façade of the Élysée. The palace, as headquarters of the administration, is an official showcase for receiving foreign heads of state and other VIPs, and for holding press conferences and receptions. The front steps have acquired a symbolic role during handovers of power and other occasions involving protocol and photo opportunities. Important guests receive the rare privilege of being accompanied by the president all the way to "the foot of the stairs." **FACING PAGE** Detail of the woodwork in the Ambassadors Room. The decorative military trophies were the work of Michel Lange the Younger to designs by Jules Michel Hardouin (nephew of great architect Jules Hardouin-Mansart). They allude to the office of Colonel General of the Royal Cavalry, held by the Count of Évreux.

THE COUNT OF ÉVREUX'S PARIS TOWN HOUSE

A lineage of two great collectors, Crozat and Mazarin, thus predated construction of the residence. The count hired architect Armand-Claude Mollet to draw up the first known plan of the mansion, published in the form of engravings in Jean Mariette's 1727 anthology of French architecture as well as Jacques-François Blondel's 1752–56 architectural treatise, indicating that the town house swiftly served as a model and a reference. Everything was already in the plan: the outbuildings, the stables and, opposite, the kitchens flanked a large rectangular courtyard that ended in a curve, and the porter's lodge was roughly where the guardhouse now stands. A slightly projecting vestibule led to the main reception room, which overlooked a terrace and garden (the only feature that no longer survives). The smaller rooms, antechambers, and bedrooms differed little from today, at least in layout, for their appearance has constantly been modified. Blondel considered it a model urban villa—"The plan of this residence is perhaps one of the best arranged and most regular presented up to this point."

Mollet was a decent architect, if unimaginative. His building had the quality of measured perfection, making it a kind of archetype. The Élysée became the model of an urban mansion during the Régence period (1715–23), with a courtyard in front and garden in back. Mollet's lack of genius led to his perfectionism. He came from a family of gardeners associated with Le Nôtre, who had sold the land. Mariette published Mollet's designs, with elevations and drawings of interiors that notably give us an idea of the ceremonial bedchamber. The main building had a second floor—left empty, since the Count of Évreux lived and entertained at the garden level—as well as an attic floor. The lack of a grand staircase didn't matter, since the owner had no intention of moving his family into the mansion. The ground floor sufficed. On the day of the first ball, in December 1720, the count repudiated his wife, Crozat's daughter, and returned her dowry—he had been enriched by Law's economic scheme, the very year France's most famous bankruptcy unfolded.

In 1722, four years after work had begun, the useful areas were almost finished, including decoration of most of the ground-floor interiors. Several sections still survive, such as the wood paneling above the fireplace in the Aides-de-Camp Room (now moved to the opposite wall). On this paneling were hung portraits and paintings glorifying the military victories of Turenne, the most famous member of the La Tour d'Auvergne family, as well as several paintings by Claude Lorrain (one of which is now in the National Gallery in London). In the main reception room (today's Ambassadors Room), decorative paneling with trophies tumbling over ribbons also dates from that period; it is the work of Michel Lange the Younger to designs by Jules Michel Hardouin (nephew of the great architect Jules Hardouin-Mansart), evoking the office of Colonel General of the Royal Cavalry (another office held by the count).

It should be kept in mind that the current names of rooms derive from former decoration or functions. They are still used not only on plans but also in the everyday speech of people who work at the palace, even though no tapestries now hang in the Tapestries Room and no military aides occupy the Aides-de-Camp Room. Nor does the Cleopatra Room feature anything recalling the

BELOW *Henri Louis de la Tour d'Auvergne, Count of Évreux* by Hyacinthe Rigaud, oil on canvas. c. 1702–04 (Kassel, Staatliche Museen, Gemäldegalerie Alte Meister). The Count of Évreux, nephew of the illustrious General Turenne, married the daughter of a wealthy financier, Antoine Crozat. The count's Paris mansion flaunted his fame and splendor, yet he never properly furnished the upstairs rooms—childless, he used only the pleasant ground-floor rooms that gave on to the garden.
FACING PAGE *Plan of the Ground Floor of the Hôtel d'Évreux, Built on the Grand Rue du Faubourg St. Honoré in Paris to Designs by Mr. Mollet, Architect to the King* by Jean Mariette, 1727.

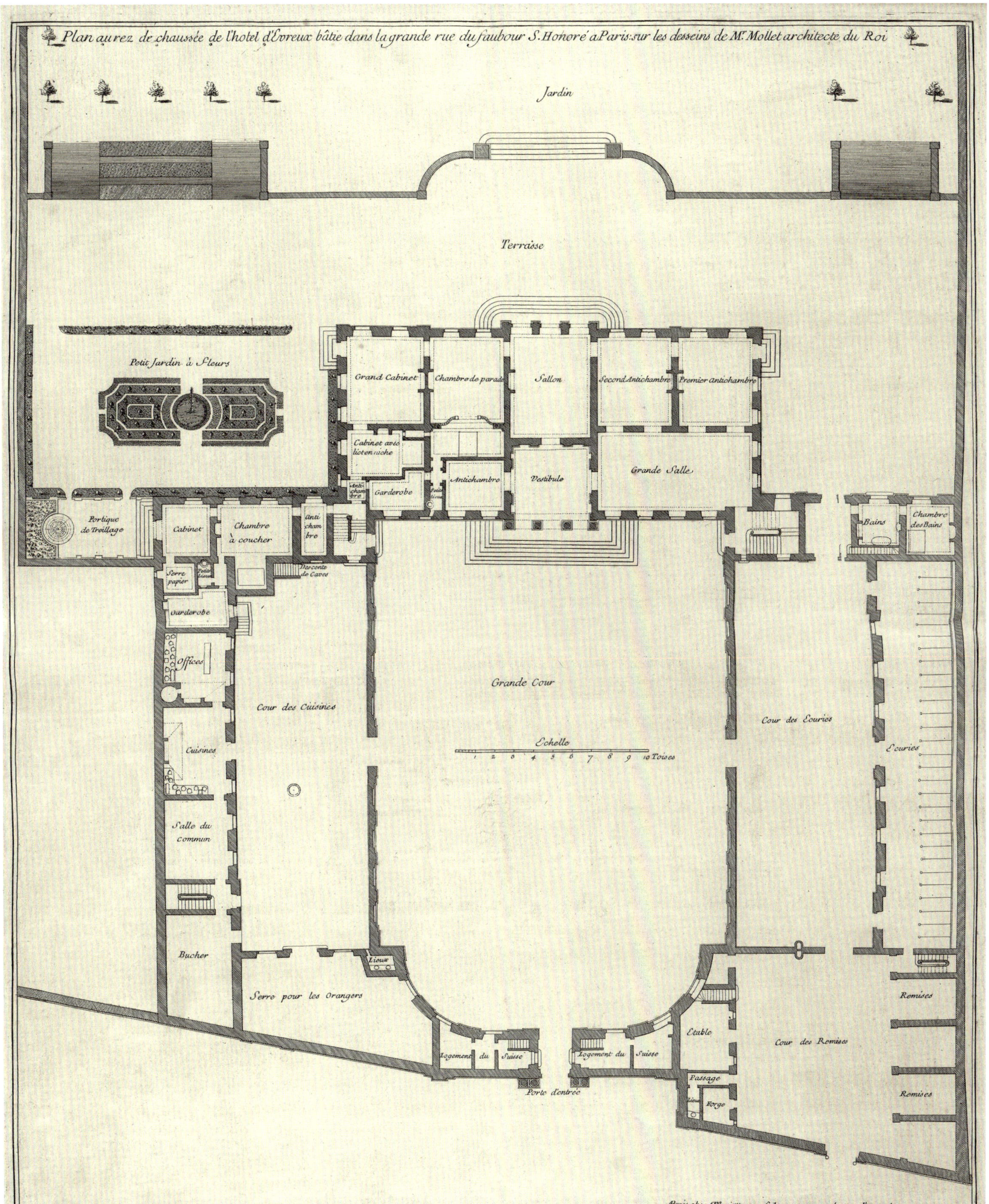
Plan au rez de chaussée de l'hotel d'Evreux bâtie dans la grande rue du faubour S. Honoré a Paris: sur les desseins de Mr. Mollet architecte du Roi
Jardin
Terrasse
Petit Jardin à Fleurs
Grand Cabinet
Chambre de parade
Sallon
Second Antichambre
Premier Antichambre
Cabinet avec lict en niche
Antichambre
Vestibule
Grande Salle
Garderobe
Portique de Treillage
Cabinet
Chambre à coucher
Anti chambre
Bains
Chambre des Bains
Serre papier
Descente de Caves
Garderobe
Offices
Cour des Cuisines
Grande Cour
Echelle
1 2 3 4 5 6 7 8 9 10 Toises
Cour des Ecuries
Ecuries
Cuisines
Salle du commun
Bucher
Serre pour les Orangers
Lieux
Logement du Suisse
Logement du Suisse
Porte d'entrée
Etable
Cour des Remises
Remises
Passage
Forge
Remises
A Paris chez Mariette rue S. Jacques aux colonnes d'Hercules

queen of Egypt (although the tapestry depicting her has fortunately survived); and it has been a very long time since the Ambassadors Room witnessed the presentation of diplomatic credentials or the awarding of a cardinal's biretta to the apostolic nuncio (as did President Auriol to Monsignor Roncalli, the future Pope John XXIII). Revampings of the Élysée never seem to affect the names of rooms—hence all these ghosts.

In the Portrait Room, an overdoor carving depicts Pallas Athena on a trophy that features a flag with a tower (*tour*), the heraldic charge of the count's family, La Tour d'Auvergne; a tower also figured on the coat of arms of Madame de Pompadour, who later bought the premises. The decorative artists rendered these military emblems with extreme elegance. Abbé Antonini, in his 1734 description of the French capital, *Mémorial de Paris,* mentioned a scientific and artistic curiosity typical of the day, namely "a moving picture, painted on copper, that depicts mechanics," which we can only imagine. When the Count of Évreux died in 1753, the Marquise of Pompadour, made Duchess of Ménars the year before, bought the residence.

BELOW *Façade of the Hôtel d'Évreux: Elevation of Courtyard Façade* by Jean-Michel Chevotet, between 1718 and 1736 (Musée Carnavalet, Paris).
FACING PAGE Detail of an overdoor panel in the Portrait Room, around 1720. Pallas Athena is seated on a trophy that includes a flag bearing a tower (*tour*), the heraldic charge of the family of the Count of Évreux (Louis Henri de la Tour d'Auvergne). Coincidentally, a tower also figured on Madame de Pompadour's coat of arms.

THE POMPADOUR ERA

Madame de Pompadour reigned over a multitude of residences, including one at Ménars, not far from Blois, overlooking the Loire; the Réservoirs estate at Versailles; a château at Champ-sur-Marne (where, in the 1900s, the Cahen d'Anvers family, which commissioned portraits from Renoir, would reinvent a "Pompadour" style); the Belleville residence at Meudon along with the nearby Pavillon de Brimborion; the Château of La Celle at Saint-Cloud; and the Hermitage at Fontainebleau (which Charles de Noailles would so skillfully redecorate in the twentieth century). All these homes were testing grounds for the development of a style that, over the years, tended toward classical features and a certain "Greek" taste—which explains the persistence of the Pompadour style down through the ages, perhaps because the original version was characterized by a perfect integration of the arts, a dialogue of all the muses, and an equality between artisans, artists, architects, ornamentalists, painters, and sculptors. The period is viewed in hindsight as the highest expression of exquisite French taste, imitated throughout the world. Reducing the Élysée to a "morganatic dwelling"—a quip attributed to Charles de Gaulle and taken up by historian Claude Dulong, who frequented the Élysée during his presidency—means underestimating the crucial role played by King Louis XV's mistress, who acted as a true "minister of cultural affairs" long before that job existed.

Madame de Pompadour dispatched a whole redecorating team to the Count of Évreux's mansion, headed by her trusted architect, Jean Cailleteau, known as Lassurance (as was his architect father, who had already adopted that "reassuring" name when working at Versailles). Also on the front line was sculptor Jacques Verberckt, who designed new marble fireplaces as well as the woodwork. Verberckt also called on luxury-goods dealer Lazare Duvaux, who delivered a large lamp and extremely rare furniture. Everyone worked for the lady who, over the years, became the king's best friend. It is probable that the superb chandeliers attributed to Jacques Caffiéri, now in the Mazarine Library of the Institut de France, were originally part of this splendid interior. Most of the renovation work involved the former ground-floor apartments of the Count of Évreux—a plan for a grand staircase, however, was never carried out. Upstairs, the rooms around the central reception room—today's Golden Room—were still in a sketchy state. Into them went part of Madame de Pompadour's famous collection of porcelain, as patron of the manufactories at Vincennes and Sèvres.

In 1762, distraught at the death of her daughter and ignored by an increasingly remote king, Madame de Pompadour admitted in a letter: "I furnished my Paris home magnificently—and enjoyed it for about two days."

Succumbing to this Paris spleen, she died two years later without having completed work on the Petit Trianon at Versailles, designed to reconcile her to the royal château. She bequeathed her Paris mansion to the king, expressing the wish—never respected—that it be attributed to the king's ten-year-old grandson, the Count of Provence (later King Louis XVIII). The masterpieces that Pompadour had assembled were auctioned off in the mansion itself, which then served as lodgings for ambassadors extraordinary.

BELOW *Portrait of Madame de Pompadour* by François Boucher, oil on canvas, 1756 (Alte Pinacotek, Bayerische Staatsgemäldesammlungen, Munich). A patron of artists, Madame de Pompadour turned her Paris mansion into a showcase of her taste in fine objects and fashionable furnishings. A different portrait of her, loaned by the Louvre, was hung in modern-style rooms by President Georges Pompidou (1969–74), expressing the idea that, despite appearances, a similar spirit and policy was being pursued under his presidency: the Élysée would promote contemporary creativity once again.
FACING PAGE Madame de Pompadour's "ceremonial bedchamber" has now become a reception room that bears her name. The pier glass was made to a design by architect Étienne-Louis Boullée around 1775.
PAGES 26-27 *The Garden and Façade of the Hôtel d'Evreux, Belonging to Madame the Marquise de Pompadour*, enhanced engraving, mid eighteenth century (Bibliothèque Nationale de France).

A COLLECTOR'S HOME

It is hardly surprising that in 1774 Nicolas Beaujon, one of the most skillful financiers of the day, became interested in the mansion that had given such perfect aristocratic expression to the Crozat fortune as well as such magnificence to the rise of the Pompadour-Marigny clan. Upon moving in, Beaujon decided to have the building redone by an architect who had worked on another of his homes (now the town hall of Issy-les-Moulineaux, outside Paris), and whose name would become legendary: Étienne-Louis Boullée. Little remains of work on the Élysée by Boullée. There is just a mirror pier, overdoor panels, and doors decorated with smoking incense burners, which he designed for Beaujon's green bedroom. A painted cupola depicting two chubby putti later vanished, to be rediscovered during the Second Empire and re-installed, somewhat touched-up—that is to say, repainted—in Napoleon III's bathroom on the ground floor. This pretty "cupola room," slightly jutting onto the Rue de l'Élysée, was used as an office by two presidential wives, Madame Giscard d'Estaing and Madame Mitterrand. Today it is occupied by the chief of staff to the president's spouse, a reminder of the opulence of tax-collector Beaujon, who had married the daughter of a certain Bontemps, a groom of the chamber to Louis XV.

Beaujon's most spectacular modification has vanished. It was a painting gallery, with overhead lighting, that ran along the private apartments overlooking the garden—which sounds marvelous. In the reception rooms, Beaujon showed off the portraits given to him by Louis XIV, by the king's two brothers (the Counts of Provence and Artois), and by the king of Sweden, whereas in his gallery he flaunted his own connoisseur's taste. The post-mortem auction of his estate in 1787 included Frans Hals's *Bohemian Woman* (now in the Louvre), Gerard ter Borch's *Woman Reading a Letter* (Royal Collection, London), Hans Holbein's *Ambassadors* (National Gallery, London), and other paintings by the likes of Guido Reni, Guercino, Poussin and Le Brun, as well as works by contemporary artists such as Greuze, Doyen, Houel, and Joseph Vernet. Even though Beaujon's period is perhaps the most overlooked, the Élysée has always exhibited works by living artists. Its walls have seen Aimé Morot's *Cavalry Charge at Rezonville* during the Franco-Prussian war (swiftly removed and now hanging in the War of 1870 Museum in Gravelotte), various loans from the Louvre, a Turner during a visit by the Queen of England and a Canaletto in honor of the president of Italy (the reverse might have been more apposite) as well as rather unappealing portraits of heads of state, removed from the Ushers Room where they looked like ghosts—General de Gaulle by Roger Chapelain-Midy and Georges Pompidou and François Mitterrand by Jean-Olivier Hucleux (such works will obviously acquire keen admirers in a century or two). These days, paintings just pass through the Élysée, leaving for other exhibition venues after a few months. They are not there to establish a "permanent" setting. For a few months visitors could see works by Maria Helena Viera da Silva and Nicolas de Staël in a tribute to the Pompidou couple, who so liked them, and two works by Simon Hantaï in the Tapestry Room. Meanwhile, *Atlantic,* a large abstract painting by Geneviève Asse was hung on the central mirror of the Ambassadors Room, facing the garden.

BELOW *Portrait of Nicolas Beaujon* by Louis Michel Van Loo, oil on canvas, 1758 (Domaine de Chaalis, Institut de France, gift of Jacquemart-André).
BOTTOM Detail of a door in the Cleopatra Room.
FACING PAGE An overdoor panel in the Ambassadors Room. Like the smoking, three-legged brazier on the detail below, the putti holding symbols of the arts were carved by Gilles Cauvet to designs by Étienne-Louis Boullée.

RIGHT A plate from the service delivered to Nicolas Beaujon in 1783 by the Sèvres porcelain manufactory. **BELOW AND FACING PAGE** Three paintings belonging to Nicolas Beaujon when he lived in the Élysée Palace: *Woman Reading a Letter* by Gerard ter Borch (Royal Collection Trust, London), *Bohemian Woman* by Frans Hals (Louvre, Paris), and *The Ambassadors* by Hans Holbein the Younger (National Gallery, London). The most lavish of French financiers was also a highly enlightened collector who installed a connoisseur's gallery in his Paris mansion.

THE BOURBON-ÉLYSÉE DURING THE REVOLUTION

Beaujon sold his mansion shortly before he died. The king bought it—but without Beaujon's collection, alas: Holbein's *Ambassadors* would have looked so good in the Louvre! The king allocated it to his cousin, the Duchess of Bourbon. (She was the sister of the Duke of Orléans who, during the Revolution, styled himself Philippe-Égalité. The duchess herself was briefly called "Citizen Truth," and was mother to the Duke of Enghien, executed by Napoleon at the Fortress of Vincennes.) The residence thus became the "Bourbon-Élysée," a Paris palace that rivaled another dwelling of the king's Bourbon cousins, in Chantilly. Architect Pierre Adrien Pâris was commissioned to alter the ground-floor apartments, replacing the boudoir with today's Silver Room and creating a bedroom with semicircular alcove (now the Library, restored to its condition under Napoleon III during Giscard d'Estaing's presidency, 1974–81).

The grounds behind the Bourbon-Élysée became a more relaxed "landscape garden" like so many others of the day, with little hamlet-like structures flanking a vast lawn. A lightning rod was installed shortly before 1789—a pointless precaution, given that the French Revolution requisitioned the Bourbon mansion and turned it into a warehouse, selling off "confiscated" furniture. However, during the Directory period (1795–99), the Duchess of Bourbon (who escaped the guillotine), recovered the property. Nonplussed, in 1797 the duchess rented it to Augustin Benoît Hovyn, a Flemish merchant who began organizing popular entertainments and activities, opening a café and a reading room. After this entrepreneur died, his daughter rented out the upper floor, divided into apartments. Although the Élysée's reputation as a "house of pleasure" long remained a butt of jokes throughout the Republican era, people forgot that it also hosted lectures on serious topics ranging from astronomy to grammar, as well as experiments in lighter-than-air craft. The tenants upstairs tended to be perfectly respectable, notably including the Marquis of Champcenetz, the widow of Marshal de Richelieu, and the parents of Alfred de Vigny.

LEFT *Auction Rooms in the Élysée Palace in 1797* by Jacques-Albert Senave, oil on canvas, 1797 (Musée Carnavalet, Paris). A label on the back of the painting indicates that this little picture "related to an Establishment ... set up in the Bourbon-Élysée to accept all kinds of art objects, with a remuneration of 50% of the price of items sold there.... But war with England having broken out, the Establishment was obliged to close."
FACING PAGE *View of the Bourbon-Élysée from the Grounds* (detail) after Henri Courvoisier-Voisin, color print before 1830 (Bibliothèque du Musée des Arts Décoratifs, Paris). This view, dating from the Restoration (when the Élysée briefly housed the Russian czar), shows the trend toward a landscape-style garden with a stream weaving across the lawn and water cascading down artificial rocks.

FROM MANSION TO PALACE

In 1805, Joachim and Caroline Murat—Napoleon's sister—bought the property and undertook major work. Caroline came from Corsica, Joachim from a small town in southwestern France, yet they turned the building into the epitome of the grand European style. The staircase with distinctive palm-leaf banister dates from this period, and was so noteworthy that Caroline posed in front of it for her portrait by François Gérard.

This staircase, with vertical laurels so instantly recognizable, has become a symbol of the Élysée, an emblem of both the place and the power—for once, the term "iconic" is no exaggeration. The stairs were originally covered with a "tiger-skin" carpet—like the saddle blanket seen in Murat's equestrian portrait by Antoine Jean Gros (now in the Louvre)—which was one of the historic references behind the 1960s style associated with interior decorator Madeleine Castaing, when ocelot skins were found in every fine home. The architects who pulled off the coup of transforming Pompadour's vestibule into an imperial entrance hall are little known: Barthélemy Vignon and Jean Thomas Thibault, the latter having worked with Boullée. But the same pair also worked on Empress Joséphine's home in Malmaison and on other Bonaparte-family dwellings.

That is when the mansion became a true palace, appropriated by the ruling clan. The apartments on the upper floors were decorated and hung with "Pompeii-style" paintings. The main reception room—today's Golden Room—gave onto a balcony decorated with imperial eagles and thunderbolts. Murat, the saber-wielding victor of the battle of Aboukir, who had been made a marshal of France and the grand duke of Berg (though not yet king of Naples), still inhabits these premises in a ghostly way, having installed a gallery (still called the Murat Room) decorated with panoramic views: Alexandre Hyacinth Dunouy, an artist notably appreciated by Caroline, depicted Trajan's column in Rome, while Joseph Xavier Bidault and Carle Vernet painted another view of Rome, and Dunouy and Vernet collaborated on a painting of Benrath Palace, all lively landscapes with figures on foot and horseback. These paintings, still in situ, were first accompanied by *The Nile at the Pyramids* and *The Seine at Neuilly*.

Bidault, a brilliant artist, was the first landscape painter to be elected to the Académie des Beaux-Arts. In 1827 his son Guillaume married Justine de Gaulle, sister of Charles de Gaulle's grandfather. This detail interested President de Gaulle, who had a Bidault from the Louvre hung in the room that then served as the cabinet office, where a landscape by Hubert Robert also hung. The entrance hall was decorated with thunderbolts and ship prows, because Murat, although always depicted on horseback, was also an admiral. The man considered a somewhat rustic parvenu was in fact an art lover, sensitive to all the latest fashions: many "modern" furnishings placed in the Murat-Élysée are still in the collection of the National Furniture Depository.

In 1810 Hippolyte Le Bas painted a watercolor of Caroline—by then queen of Naples—in the Silver Room, as that room still looks today thanks to skillful restoration. Even though it cannot rival the Platinum Room designed by Percier and Fontaine in 1802–04—and hung with paintings by Anne-Louis Girodet—for the Casa del Labrador in Aranjuez, Spain, the Silver Room is a valuable example of the Empire style. The swan-necked armchairs, upholstered in red for

FACING PAGE *Caroline Murat, Queen of Naples* by François Gérard, oil on canvas (Châteaux de Versailles et de Trianon). Napoleon's sister is shown on the grand staircase of the Élysée, built by architects Barthélemy Vignon and Jean Thomas Thibault in 1810.

Caroline but redone sometime after 1813 in mauve (the current state), were unaware that some day they would have as neighbors, just a few doors down, an ostrich cocktail bar designed by Claude and François Lalanne (a whimsical item acquired for the Pompidous' dining room designed by Pierre Paulin). In the Murats' day, the clock featuring "the chariot of Faithfulness driven by Cupid" played only a decorative role.

Once the Murats left to rule in Naples (where Dunouy's fine landscapes still hang), the palace became an imperial residence, housing Empress Joséphine and her daughter Hortense (as fondly recalled by Hortense's son, the future Napoleon III). Napoleon himself often stayed at the "Napoleon-Élysée," preferring this comfortable dwelling to the "grim grandeur" of the Tuileries Palace, despite renovation work by Percier and Fontaine. Once Napoleon divorced Joséphine, she left the Élysée, taking the Italian paintings hung by the Murats to her Malmaison home. In 1812 the new empress, Marie-Louise, had apartments in the Élysée fitted out for her newborn son, styled the king of Rome—the woodwork was padded so that the imperial heir would not hurt himself.

During the Hundred Days War in 1815, Napoleon stayed at the Élysée, sleeping in a bedroom with an elegant tripod washstand (a small yet valuable furnishing that he took into exile on Saint Helena, now owned by the Louvre and symbolically included in the first exhibition in the Gallery of Time in the new Louvre-Lens). This tripod epitomized the Empire style, which continued to spread around the world well after the emperor's death in 1821, haunting the Élysée down to de Gaulle's day. On June 22, 1815, the defeated Napoleon signed his abdication in favor of his son, Napoleon II, in the Élysée's Silver Room. And then he left the palace by the garden door, as de Gaulle would do in 1969, without awaiting the results of the referendum that obliged the president to resign—the Silver Room is a place of farewells.

It was in this room, used as an office, that Napoleon's nephew studied the file on Operation Rubicon, the coup d'état of December 2, 1851, which carried him to the imperial throne under the name of Napoleon III. Victor Hugo, who had accepted the man's hospitality when he was still president of the Second Republic, later attacked Napoleon III in his poetry collection *Châtiments* (Castigations).

During the Restoration, the Élysée briefly housed the Russian czar, followed by the Duke of Wellington, before it was allocated to the nephew of Louis XVIII, the dashing Duke of Berry. In 1816, the duke married Maria Carolina of Bourbon-Sicily, marking the start of an elegant period of masked balls, parties,

ABOVE Detail of an overdoor panel in the Silver Room. The lyre suggests that it was used as a music room in the days of Caroline Murat, Napoleon's sister.
FACING PAGE Delicately gilded in white gold, the Silver Room has retained its original wood paneling. Here a winged putto holding a torch and palm branch stands above a pier table with flower box.

LEFT *Caroline Murat, Queen of Naples, in the Silver Boudoir of the* Élysée *Palace* by Hippolyte Le Bas, watercolor, 1810 (Château de Mouchy). This painting shows the decoration of the Silver Room during the First Empire. Its carved woodwork was gilded with white gold and painted with putti and trophies. The furniture by Jacob Desmalter, originally upholstered in red, was covered with lilac-colored silk after 1813. This is the room where Napoleon I signed his abdication on June 22, 1815, and where Napoleon III prepared his coup d'état of December 2, 1851.

and other "bashes," reviving the aura of a frivolous, entertaining court. In a sign of the times, the tiger-skin carpet on the main staircase was replaced by one imitating a flowery lawn. The Élysée set the tone with its warm, fruit-wood furniture and walls lined in blue or light green silk, with gold-and-crystal objets d'art.

When the Duke of Berry was assassinated in February 1820, his widow moved to the Tuileries Palace, where she gave birth to a son—first styled Duke of Bordeaux, later Count of Chambord—who became the darling of Chateaubriand and the legitimists. The Élysée was then used to host guests, even after the Orléans family ascended to the French throne in 1830—King Louis-Philippe occasionally lent the empty premises to foreign princes passing through Paris. He considered it a family home, since it had belonged to his aunt, the Duchess of Orléans.

When Louis-Philippe was forced to abdicate in 1848, the Élysée became the property of the new republic. It first served as a venue for concerts and lectures designed to educate the people, then became the residence of the first president of the Second Republic: Louis-Napoleon Bonaparte. For him, too, the Élysée was a family home—which also became the center of government for the first time.

A true restoration campaign was thereupon launched, led by the head of the Furniture Depository, Germain Delavigne. His redecoration hinted at the imminent return of empire, with the installation of Robert Lefevre's large portrait of Empress Joséphine, a version of Jacques Louis David's *Bonaparte Crossing the Alps,* and busts of the emperor's relatives. In 1851 gas lighting was installed and a canopy was erected over the porch, soon replaced by a larger one to protect visitors from the rain (becoming the "monkey cage" during Sadi Carnot's presidency, used as a cloakroom for major receptions). Louis-Napoleon Bonaparte, still styled the "Prince-President" and still a bachelor, hosted big parties and received visitors in the company of his intelligent cousin, Mathilde Bonaparte.

BELOW Louis-Napoleon Bonaparte, as president of the Second Republic, is shown arriving at the Élysée on December 20, 1848, in an engraving published in *The Illustrated London News.* The mansion had been decreed the nation's presidential residence on December 12 of that year. Louis-Napoleon Bonaparte moved into private apartments on the ground floor.
RIGHT *The Bourbon-Élysée in Paris,* plate from the historic Fontainebleau dinner service, painted by L. R. Lyngbye from a gouache design by J. B. J. van Marcke, 1842 (Château de Fontainebleau).

PALAIS
de
l'ÉLYSÉE-BOURBON
à Paris.

ELYSEE NAPOLEON

MAJOR WORK UNDER NAPOLEON III

In 1852, the Tuileries Palace became the official residence of the new emperor, Napoleon III. He did not forsake the Élysée, however, allocating it to his Spanish fiancée, Eugénie de Montijo, and her mother (who, as an old friend of Prosper Mérimée, would spend the rest of her days there, never bringing herself to return to Madrid). There thus began the construction of another palace that enveloped the first. The service wings flanking the main courtyard were redesigned with inner courtyards and passages; the façade on Rue du Faubourg Saint-Honoré, the stables, and the buildings on the Avenue Marigny side were redone; the Rue de l'Élysée (initially named Avenue de la Reine Hortense) was laid out and English-style houses built there. Architect Joseph Eugène Lacroix gave the Élysée its current appearance, so successfully integrated into the eighteenth-century one that it is sometimes difficult to distinguish the two strata. In Lacroix, Napoleon III had chosen a now-forgotten architect who was linked to the emperor's personal entourage, being the son of a servant to Napoleon's mother and the brother of Hortense Lacroix Cornu, with whom the emperor had grown up. Hortense was one of the few women who dared speak to the emperor plainly, and she hosted an intellectual salon that rivaled Mathilde Bonaparte's. She married a talented pupil of the great artist Ingres, Sébastien Cornu, who had republican leanings yet decorated the Élysée chapel with religious figures. Lacroix was so trusted that he didn't bother to request administrative authorizations—the emperor himself was overseeing what might become a second residence.

The obscure Lacroix can be credited with the glorious triumphal arch marking the street entrance, its twinned columns punctuating an austere screen and distantly recalling the great gate at Les Invalides (which would have a final incarnation in 1900 in the main entrance to the Petit Palais).

FACING PAGE, TOP *Paris in All its Splendor: The Élysée Palace (Garden Façade)*, lithograph by Eugène Cicéri after Félix Benoist (Bibliothèque Nationale de France, Paris). Emperor Napoleon III and Empress Eugénie can be seen strolling in the grounds.
FACING PAGE, BOTTOM The "Napoleon-Élysée," as it became known on December 2, 1852, pictured in *The Illustrated London News*. In 1856, architect Joseph Eugène Lacroix devised a monumental entrance composed of a gated arch and two side passages for pedestrians, orchestrated around two sets of double Corinthian columns on a single base. The archivolt, inscribed with the new name of the palace, was crowned by the imperial coat of arms carved by Ovide Savreux.
RIGHT The main courtyard of the Élysée where a new iron-and-zinc awning, flanked by slender-columned galleries of glass, was installed along the façade in 1854.

After 1857, Lacroix attacked the main body of the building, which had remained untouched since it was built. The entire interior was stripped in three years. Lacroix had the woodwork carefully removed; damaged sections were copied and adjusted; everything from floors to ceilings was taken apart and put back together. Casts were made of the cornices and friezes—ornamental sculptor Ovide Savreux made sure everything retained an eighteenth-century air. New doors were created by sacrificing panels such as the one to the right of the fireplace in the Portrait Room, but the original layout was respected; mirrors were replaced (henceforth in a single sheet), and the bronzework on the balcony was redone, decorated with crowns and bees (still there). The Murat Room was pierced with windows that today give onto the kitchen (built later), several of the large landscapes were removed, and overdoors were embellished with the monogram of Napoleon and Eugénie. Rooms dating from Madame de Pompadour's day were enriched with decorative details in *carton pierre* (papier mâché that imitates stone), fluted columns were graced with tendrils, and everything was subtly highlighted, gilded, recomposed. The woodwork was done in pine, designed to be painted; oak was used only for certain features of the casements. Savreux produced models of door handles bearing the monogram "N." In 1861, the doors were fitted with a mark of modernity: protective finger-plates. The authentic eighteenth-century decoration didn't vanish, but was transformed into a new "Louis XVI–Empress" style, which blossomed upstairs where inventiveness reigned in the form of beribboned bows, beaded borders, and scrolling foliage and flowers.

For the so-called Semicircular Salon, Charles Chaplin painted overdoors in the style of François Boucher. The fireplaces—some of which, in blue Turquin marble, were very Louis XV in look—were replaced by copies of Versailles models: the Aides-de-Camp Room was given a replica of the one in Louis XV's bedchamber and the Grand Salon (where cabinet meetings are held today) copied the fireplace in the royal council chamber. What would become the Golden Room upstairs was given a somewhat enlarged, if correctly proportioned, version of the fireplace designed by Ange-Jacques Gabriel in 1747 for the dauphin's bedroom, and the Empress's Room imitated the fireplace in Louis XVI's library. The Silver Room, being a sanctuary of the First Empire, remained almost intact, although the paint was somewhat touched-up. A new Élysée was thereby superimposed on the old one, merging with it and creating an ambiguity that long endured.

The two masterpieces of this composite style were the Golden Room, the pride of this reinvented palace, and the Mirror Room (formerly the empress's bathroom). The Golden Room, although never intended to host an abstract painting by Pierre Soulages or modern blue furniture by Pierre Paulin, has always harmoniously valorized them, demonstrating that the spectacular and long-disparaged Second-Empire style can, in fact, hack it. In 1861 the decorative painter was Jean-Louis Godon. The Golden Room proclaimed a style full of allusions and quotations, like some dazzling conversation: a tapestry was enhanced by a large frame (today removed) and golden panels were enlivened with arabesques from which sprang dancing women, putti with baskets of flowers, and garlands of roses. The initials "N" and "E," set into medallions, glittered in the sunlight.

The bathroom, also decorated by Godon in association with Chaplin, re-employed the ideas and patterns found in a bathroom in the Royal Wardrobe, a refined gem that had been installed by Intendent-General Pierre Élisabeth de Fontanieu and then given painted-glass decoration by his successor.

FACING PAGE View of the Ambassadors Room. The fireplace, installed in 1860, is a copy of the one in the royal council chamber at Versailles.

FACING PAGE The "Louis XVI-Empress style" was based on elegant sources: the Mirror Room, decorated by Jean-Louis Godon in conjunction with Charles Chaplin, was inspired by the famous bathroom of the director of the Royal Wardrobe, which had been transferred to Fontainebleau but today is back in its original setting in the Hôtel de la Marine in Paris.
BELOW Napoleon III paying a visit to Sultan Abdulaziz in the Élysée Palace in 1867. In fact, the emperor allocated the palace to illustrious visitors to the second International Exposition held in Paris.

King Louis-Philippe then had it transferred to the Château of Fontainebleau when the Royal Wardrobe on Place de la Concorde was assigned to the naval ministry. This "Mirror Room" was placed back in situ in 1996—meanwhile, its Second-Empire version in the Élysée is now used as an office, with piles of folders occasionally sitting on what was the bathtub. Chaplin, more Boucher in style than ever, painted mythological subjects based on Diana, Leda, and, of course, Venus (characters straight out of Offenbach's 1864 operetta, *La Belle Hélène*). The empress's vast canopy bed, adorned with emerald drapes, once occupied what is now the president's everyday office. (The bed is currently in the Second Empire Museum in Compiègne.) The colossal renovation work was only completed in 1867, in time for the International Exposition. The imperial couple entertained in the renovated palace, where they received foreign guests such as the czar of Russia, the sultan of Turkey, and the viceroy of Egypt, yet they continued to live in the Tuileries Palace. The impact of the Élysée as transformed by Napoleon III was such that it still survives, much like Baron Haussmann's urban design still dominates Paris itself. The recent restoration had to confront this difficulty. By retaining the main structures added by architect Lacroix, it was possible to restore the freshness of eighteenth-century woodwork where it survived, while reviving, elsewhere, the charm of the Second-Empire apartments.

UNDER THE THIRD REPUBLIC

At the start of the Third Republic (1870–1940), President Adolphe Thiers only briefly resided in the Élysée. His vast art collection could never fit into its narrow walls. But in 1874 the new president, General Patrice de Mac-Mahon—whom Napoleon III had made duke of Magenta—installed the presidency in the palace, only too happy to move his family there and occupy the emperor's former bedroom.

Lacroix, the architect, was killed by a train in Le Vésinet station in 1873, so he was replaced by Eugène Auguste Debressenne, who completed work on the indispensible Ballroom, which immediately proved too small but could be used as a large dining room (to plans by Lacroix) next to the Murat Room. The organic growth of the palace thus began along that Avenue de Marigny side—in 1879, during the presidency of Jules Grévy, a glass conservatory, or "Winter Garden," was added, creating a transition between the interior and the grounds outside, yet was so dark that no plants ever thrived. President Sadi Carnot (1887–94) enveloped the useless Winter Garden by building, beyond it, a real reception hall (designed by Debressenne's successor, Adrien Chancel).

Electricity was installed under President Carnot and was extended to the floor above under Faure (1895–99). The "Sun President," as the latter was dubbed, had fifty-six imitation candles wired into the chandelier in the main reception room. The telephone arrived, as an experimental curiosity, as early as Grévy's term (1879–87). The Tapestry Room was thus named under President Fallières, in 1907, with the arrival of the tapestry series *The Story of Scipio*. A ceiling painting commissioned from Henri Gervex was never installed—the hook for the chandelier would have run straight through the allegory *France Welcoming Abundance*. The Tapestry Room, although constantly traversed, has no specific use. President Sarkozy (2007–12) had placed the badge of the

LEFT *The Shah of Persia Visits France in July 1873* by Frédéric Théodore Lix, engraving published in *Le Monde Illustré*. The reception for Shah Nazir al-Din given by President Mac-Mahon was held in what is today the Pompadour Room. It was in September 1874 that the Élysée Palace was permanently designated as the residence of the president of France.
FACING PAGE, TOP The Semicircular Salon renamed the Pompadour Room, 1925. Photo: Meurisse news agency (Bibliothèque Nationale de France, Paris).
FACING PAGE, BOTTOM *France Welcoming Abundance: Sketch for a Ceiling in the* Élysée *Palace* by Henri Gervex, oil on canvas, c. 1907 (Musée Carnavalet, Paris).

Order of the Golden Fleece, awarded to him by the king of Spain, in a little display case there. Today the room hosts *Diabolo,* a carpet by Elisabeth Garouste and Mattia Bonetti, and pier tables and lamps by sculptor Philippe Anthonioz. As the son of Geneviève Anthonioz de Gaulle, Anthonioz was hardly awed by the place, and his furnishings are a particularly good symbol of continuity at the Élysée in so far as they were designed for the private apartments of President Mitterrand, a political adversary of de Gaulle.

The Cleopatra Room is another point of passage between reception rooms and private rooms. It, too, has never been of much use. It earned its name during the Third Republic from a tapestry woven to a design by Charles Natoire. But even calling it something else would change little. The dominant tone of the furnishings, placed there during the height of the Third Republic, is the Empire style, which accords with the idea of a somewhat austere yet swaggering France. This 1910 Empire style is perhaps the least loved of all—which means it is certain to make a comeback.

During World War II, the National Furniture Depository shipped the Élysée's treasures to Aubusson. A freeze set in, despite a few attempts to refurbish the building for Admiral Darlan and, toward the end of the war, for Marshal Pétain, who never came to Paris. Uninhabited, closed, the building slumbered—although it occasionally hoisted a sinister flag.

RIGHT Sadi Carnot, president of France from 1887 to 1894, and his brilliant wife, Cécile (daughter of socialist economist Charles Brook Dupont-White), seen in the Élysée's new Ballroom.

BELOW President Poincaré leaving the Élysée in a horse-drawn carriage on January 1, 1914. Photo Rol news agency (Bibliothèque Nationale de France, Paris).
FACING PAGE, TOP The Prince of Wales arriving at the front porch of the palace in a car, July 23, 1912. Photo Rol news agency (Bibliothèque Nationale de France, Paris).
FACING PAGE, BOTTOM U.S. General John Pershing arriving at the Élysée in a Renault, 1921. Photo: Meurisse news agency (Bibliothèque Nationale de France, Paris).

Rol 22171
143415

MEU 92372
C 20427

BELOW Vacuuming the carpet on the porch of the Élysée Palace, 1921–22. Photo by Félix Peaucou (private collection). The large glass structure that served as a cloakroom since Sadi Carnot's presidency , dubbed the "monkey cage," was demolished in 1947.
FACING PAGE Winston Churchill leaving the Élysée in 1925. Photo: Meurisse news agency (Bibliothèque Nationale de France, Paris).

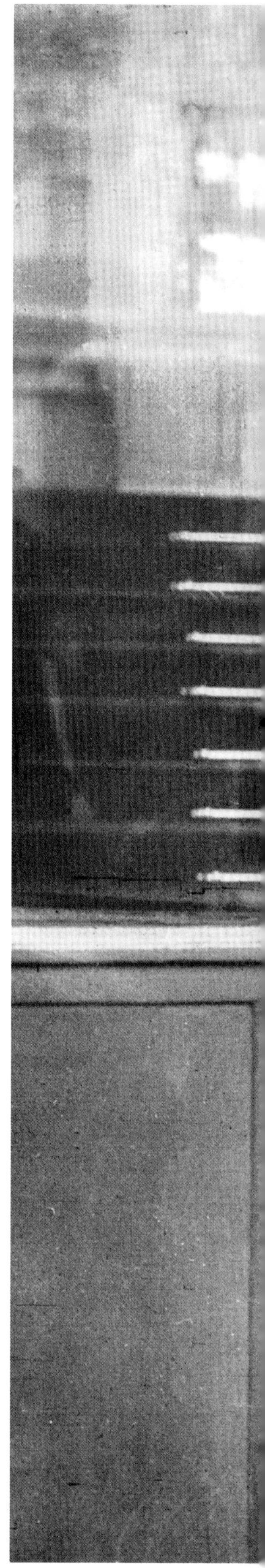

The Ballroom

The Ballroom would become one of the most essential, and most popular, places in the palace, hosting inauguration ceremonies for new presidents, state dinners, Christmas celebrations, and press conferences. Since it is the largest room in the palace, this was where President de Gaulle recorded his TV interviews—cameras of the day required lots of room and distance, but to stress the personal nature of the interview, breaking with the pomp of press-conference ritual, imitation wood paneling was erected to imitate a more private room. A photograph shows this stage set, which superimposed a fake eighteenth-century décor on a republican Ballroom. Today, this role is played by a backdrop of white prefabricated panels, replacing the silly artifice of a blue curtain that some ministers continue to place behind themselves, naively hoping they won't be associated with ritzy woodwork (but regularly resulting in wide-angle photos showing the original woodwork sticking out behind the blue curtain, thereby giving the lie to this childish refusal to accept French heritage and history).

In 1889, for the hundredth anniversary of the French Revolution, a wing of iron and brick was erected in a matter of months, encroaching on the trees. (At the same time, girders were inserted to reinforce the floors of the main historic sections.) This long box, tacked onto the old building, would be opened up in 1984 under President François Mitterrand, in an attempt to lighten it: the red and gold hues and heavy decoration—regularly increased and enriched up to 1896—created a somewhat stifling atmosphere in what was a large, vast gallery. The Ballroom, associated with the most ceremonial occasions, plunged guests into a kind of Third-Republic stupor. When medals were awarded, everyone took on the royal red hue of the old carpet. The heavily patterned, worn-out rug looked as though it had witnessed the lying-in-state of President Félix Faure, who died in the Élysée in 1899. (It is well known that he died while entertaining his mistress, Madame Steinheil.) But this cherry-colored carpet with white flowers in fact dates from 2007, copying a pattern of 1894. In 1932, the weavers of Aubusson had benefited from a refurbishment of the Ballroom by upholstering its new furniture, signaling the revival of the historic tapestry manufactory. Recently it was the turn of their eternal rivals in Felletin to supply over ten thousand square feet of carpet, radically changing the appearance of this part of the building. Indeed, it was the historic Pinton firm in Felletin that won the latest contract, even if it resorted to looms in the Manufacture Royale du Parc back in Aubusson, which employed traditional perforated-card techniques.

The restoration undertaken by President Emmanuel Macron, and his wife, Brigitte Macron, has given this décor a subtle gray and gold hue that should age well—an idea suggested by interior designer Isabelle Stanislas, who has worked with the National Furniture Depository. Stanislas also deserves credit for revealing three handsome ceiling panels, glowingly painted on copper by Guillaume Dubufe (titled *Art, The Republic Upholds Peace,* and *Science*); she furthermore protected the fine tapestries from the series of *The Story of Esther.* Music has returned to this quiet, peaceful room, which now hosts concerts (thus requiring the rental of a piano, since the palace apparently doesn't yet own one).

BELOW President Charles de Gaulle interviewed by journalist Michel Droit on April 10, 1969. A film set of imitation wood panels had been installed (above which the vaulted ceiling can be glimpsed) in order to give a less ostentatious feel to the conversation.
FACING PAGE Cleaning the Grand Ballroom at the Élysée, 1921–22, photo by Félix Peaucou (private collection). Built to coincide with the International Exposition of 1889, the Ballroom hosts official ceremonies ranging from presidential inaugurations to state receptions, state dinners, Christmas and New Year celebrations, press conferences, and medal-awarding ceremonies.

ABOVE An official dinner during the presidency of Charles de Gaulle, June 1959.
LEFT The orchestra playing at a reception given for President and Mrs. Kennedy on May 31, 1961.
FACING PAGE Detail of the ceiling of the Ballroom with its monumental chandeliers (fitted with imitation candles in 1961).

FACING PAGE During a meeting of the North Atlantic Treaty Organization in Paris in 1955, the heads of government of NATO countries were invited to a formal dinner at the Élysée. RIGHT Queen Elizabeth II during a state dinner at the Élysée Palace in April 1957. She replied in French to the welcoming address by President René Coty (seated, right). Behind the president is Prince Philip, Duke of Edinburgh.

ABOVE U.S. President Dwight Eisenhower (center) and French President René Coty (right) in the Ambassadors Room after a dinner in December 1957. On the left is President of the Council of Ministers Félix Gaillard.
LEFT Tables are set and staff is in livery for a dinner in the Ballroom around 1950.
FACING PAGE, TOP The Ballroom with its heavy red drapes and Gobelins tapestries of *The Story of Esther*, after Jean-François de Troy.
FACING PAGE, BOTTOM LEFT President de Gaulle's place at an official dinner in June 1959.
FACING PAGE, BOTTOM RIGHT A bygone lifestyle: cigars and cigarettes offered after dinner at the Élysée in the 1950s.

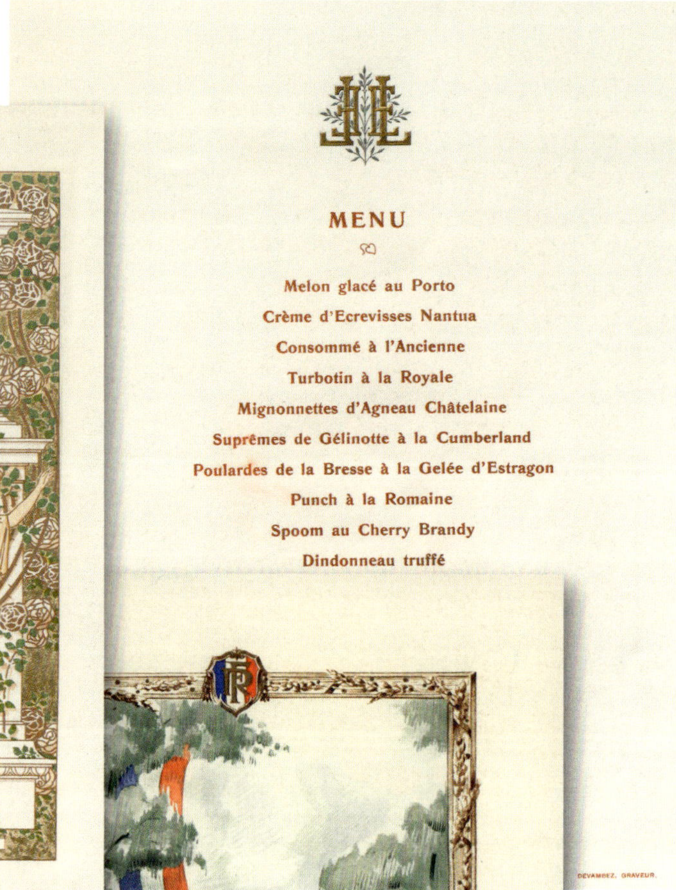

MENU

Melon glacé au Porto
Crème d'Ecrevisses Nantua
Consommé à l'Ancienne
Turbotin à la Royale
Mignonnettes d'Agneau Châtelaine
Suprêmes de Gélinotte à la Cumberland
Poulardes de la Bresse à la Gelée d'Estragon
Punch à la Romaine
Spoom au Cherry Brandy
Dindonneau truffé

DEVAMBEZ, GRAVEUR.

Potage Tortue Claire
Mousseline de Volaille
Croustades à la Montglas
Truites Saumonées de la Loire
Agneau de Pauillac Massenet
Suprêmes de Gélinottes
Noisettes de Foie gras à la Gelée
Spooms au Clicquot
Granités à la Mandarinette
Poulardes de la Bresse truffées à la Broche
Petits Jambons glacés au Marsala
Salade Montfermeil
Asperges en Branches sauce Crème
Champignons de Rosée à la Meunière
Glace Francillon

Lenepveu
Mozart
Haendel
Massenet
Gounod
Wallace
Th. Dubois

MUSIQUE DE LA GARDE RÉPUBLICAINE

The history of the Élysée can also be traced through menus of official luncheons and dinners. The allegorical illlustrations favored by the Third Republic (1870–1940) were replaced in the late 1950s by black-and-white engravings of the palace, which gave way to artworks by French artists in the years 1970–2000. The past three presidential terms have favored more straightforward emblems of the French Republic.

ABOVE (LEFT TO RIGHT, TOP TO BOTTOM) Menu of a dinner given by President Loubet for King Alfonso XIII of Spain on May 30, 1905; Concordia menu of the dinner given by President Poincaré for King George V of Great Britain on April 21, 1914; menu of the dinner given by President Lebrun for King George VI on July 19, 1938; menu of the dinner given on April 9, 1957 for the state visit by Queen Elizabeth II.

FACING PAGE (TOP TO BOTTOM) Menu of the dinner given by President de Gaulle on March 9, 1966, for France's elite administrative corps; menu of the dinner given by President Mitterrand for the president of the People's Republic of China on November 9, 1987. The painting by Maurice Estève, *Bélasse* (1966), adorned many menus of that period. Menu of the dinner given by President Mitterrand for Senegalese president Abdou Diouf on April 8, 1994, illustrated by Gilles Marey's *Lemons* (1993). The strings and tassels are in the colors of the guest country.

Velouté Germiny

Bar froid à la Parisienne

Selle d'agneau de Pauillac rôtie

Haricots verts au beurre

Parfait Trianon

Riesling 1961
Château Haut-Brion 1959
Heidsieck Monopole 1959

Etuvée de homard
au parfum de Saint-Jacques

Caneton nantais à la Sévillane

Pommes moulées à l'ancienne

Salade

Glace ardéchoise

Corton-Charlemagne 1984 (Bouchard Père & Fils)
Château Fonreque 1983
René Lalou 1979

Feuilleté d'oeuf poché au caviar

Gigot des Alpilles vert-pré rôti au romarin

Etuvée d'artichauts aux gnocchi

Fromages

Crème glacée chocolat et vanille

Jus de fruits
Sancerre blanc (C. Salmon) 1991
Château Poujeaux 1978
Louise Pommery 1987

RIGHT President de Gaulle giving a speech during an official reception for Prince Rainier and Princess Grace of Monaco on October 13, 1959. After a dinner for one hundred and thirty guests, the Ballroom hosted a performance by the Paris Opéra ballet company to music by Debussy, Tchaikovsky, and Lalo.

ABOVE Jacqueline Kennedy and Yvonne de Gaulle at an official reception given on May 31, 1961.
LEFT President John Kennedy and First Lady Jacqueline Kennedy climbing the steps to the Élysée Palace.
FACING PAGE Indian Prime Minister Jawaharlal Nehru and his daughter Indira Gandhi received by President Georges Pompidou and his wife Claude in September 1962.

On August 24, 1944, General de Gaulle entered Paris. The Élysée was liberated by the Republican Guard, but France's national hero decided to move, temporarily, into the Brienne mansion, headquarters of the Ministry of War.

President Vincent Auriol (1947–54) and his wife Michelle (the daughter of a master glazier) played a major role in restoring the Élysée after the Liberation, during the fleeting Fourth Republic. They first undertook a major renovation project that sought to recover the purity of Mollet's original design for the Count of Évreux. That meant eliminating the light fixtures in the courtyard, the glass cage on the porch, and the disfiguring clock on the pediment (a modern touch adopted by many châteaux in France, perhaps in envy of train stations). Two absurd windows that flanked the one in the center of the façade were filled in, while the entrance hall was made transparent though large, frameless windows, a good idea that has not gone out of fashion. Appreciation of the Napoleon III style was then at its lowest. Everything needed to be revamped as a sign that a new era had begun—postwar fashion called for new decoration.

Cabinet meetings were held in what was called the Semicircular Salon, and the chapel was turned into offices. A handsome room with cupola was allocated to the head of the secretariat. The presidential office remained on the ground floor, with the Silver Room being used as an extra presidential annex.

Since the "monkey cage" had been demolished, an underground cloakroom had to be built, employing a dumbwaiter system perhaps inspired by Thomas Jefferson's still-functioning system in Monticello; it is notably used for official dinners entailing a great number of guests. On the other side of the wall was the Count of Evreux's bedroom with a curved alcove flanked by two columns, where it was decided to hang a tapestry designed by Simon Vouet, *Elijah on the Chariot of Fire,* seen in so many photographs that it had to be urgently removed to avoid being completely burned out by the photographer's flash. In the Bible, the prophet Elijah, on being carried up to heaven, designated Eliseus (or Elisha) as his successor—but that was no reason to sacrifice one of the finest tapestries from the set of *The Story of the Old Testament,* woven for Louis XIII's Louvre Palace (and thus totally anachronistic in this setting).

The Auriol period was crucial because it established the link with the National Furniture Depository and marked the first signs of openness to major contemporary designers such as Jules Leleu and André Arbus. Bright damasks were chosen to enliven the old upstairs rooms, such as Empress Eugénie's bathroom, where there was no question of removing the mirrors. President René Coty (1954–59) put the Auriols' modern additions into store, merely adding some new fabrics so that France wouldn't be shamed by the first visit of Queen Elizabeth II and the Duke of Edinburgh in 1957. Thus vanished the charming, if faded, fabrics familiar to Empress Eugénie—and probably Queen Victoria. Coty also refurbished the Golden Room (although he didn't use it for his office), as though France anticipated what was coming.

The revolution carried out by de Gaulle in 1959 was similar to the one effected by Louis XIV when he decided, as late as 1701, to place his bedchamber in the central reception room of Versailles. At the Élysée, the office of the president of the new Fifth Republic would no longer be on the ground floor, but would

BELOW, TOP First Lady Michelle Auriol with her daughter-in-law Jacqueline Auriol and two grandchildren in the Golden Room, photographed by François Kollar around 1948–50 (Médiathèque de l'Architecture et du Patrimoine, Charenton-le-Pont).

BELOW, BOTTOM President Charles de Gaulle posing in the Library in 1959 for his official portrait by fashion photographer Jean-Marie Marcel. Some of the pictures from that shoot showed de Gaulle in full uniform, others in military evening dress—the latter, more stylish, version prevailed.

FACING PAGE President de Gaulle during a press conference in the Ballroom in 1965.

RIGHT Actress Brigitte Bardot leaving the Élysée after a dinner given by President de Gaulle in December 1967. She broke the cocktail-dress tradition by wearing black pants and a long tunic with braiding, described by André Malraux as "frogged pajamas."

occupy the finest, most richly decorated room, in the center. (In a later interview about the restoration of Louis XIV's bedchamber at Versailles, President Giscard d'Estaing stressed the lateness of Louis's move in 1701, suggesting that the king had long thought about it—a comment made by a president who decided *not* to work in the Élysée's large, central room.) The Cressent desk that had been used by Félix Faure was thus installed there, along with a discreet emblem of authority, one of six Empire-era Bouillotte (or shaded) lamps made by Guillaume-Martin Biennais. Until recently, one or two of those lamps always featured in the presidential office, with others in the prime minister's office at the Matignon Palace. Given their resemblance to one with a green shade seen in a painting by Jacques Louis David, *The Emperor Napoleon in his Study at the Tuileries* (National Gallery, Washington, D.C.), they are thought to be Napoleon's desk lamps—a symbolic item complementing a Savonnerie carpet made for Louis XIV. All regional prefects subsequently desired an Empire-style Bouillotte lamp—never were so many made as under de Gaulle. Cabinet meetings were thereafter moved to the kitchen that the Auriols had decorated by Leleu, with walls lined in green silk.

The rooms flanking the president's office were allocated to his closest assistants, namely his chief of staff and secretary general. The secretary general's office then acquired the armchairs that became popular when Giscard d'Estaing conducted his "fireside" TV chats there; these elegant eighteenth-century models were neither gilded nor stamped by a historic furniture maker, reflecting Giscard's philosophy about his role—the rejection of an historic provenance and a famous name was probably intended as a sign of simplicity, yet seemed a little too calculated to be appreciated for its true value.

Under de Gaulle's presidency (1959–69), the ebb of Napoleon III furnishings was soon followed by a flow of Empire furniture, some of which came from the Château of Versailles, others from the Château of Fontainebleau. There was little concern for provenance, whereas today the National Furniture Depository seeks to relocate its stock of furniture (some of which had long been in the Élysée) in grand French châteaux. De Gaulle, however, wanted "Madame de Pompadour's Élysée" to be more virile; he wanted to return to Murat and grandeur, to solid government.

The ground-floor rooms beyond the ones that led upstairs were employed for receptions. The use of and movement through rooms were thus made more rational, although no restoration was carried out during de Gaulle's ten-year term. That period forged an image of a palace furnished in a strict and somewhat austere pomp, with a few sparkling items of furniture that reflected the nation's history.

President Georges Pompidou (1969–74) took a different tack. In small, tactful touches, he breathed a needed modernity into the Gaullist palace. During his short term, Pompidou set the stage for a new style without ill-treating the building. Although his secretary general, Édouard Balladur, couldn't resist the temptation of a "grand" roll-top desk, the rest of the palace staff was open to modern design—if not all at once and not everywhere. The president's office was furnished with Boulle medal cabinets (now in the Furniture Depository) that served as the background for decades of photo opportunities. Some plain-wood Régence armchairs from the office next door were also moved in, creating a disparate ensemble whose sole unity was its gathering of a few great examples of French historic furniture, thereby expressing—as under de Gaulle—a sense of grandeur (even

FACING PAGE Like his predecessors Félix Faure, Émile Loubet, and Armand Fallières, President Charles de Gaulle worked on a Régence-period desk that is now legendary. Made by Charles Cressent around 1750, the five-drawer writing desk features gilt-bronze busts of warriors on the corners.

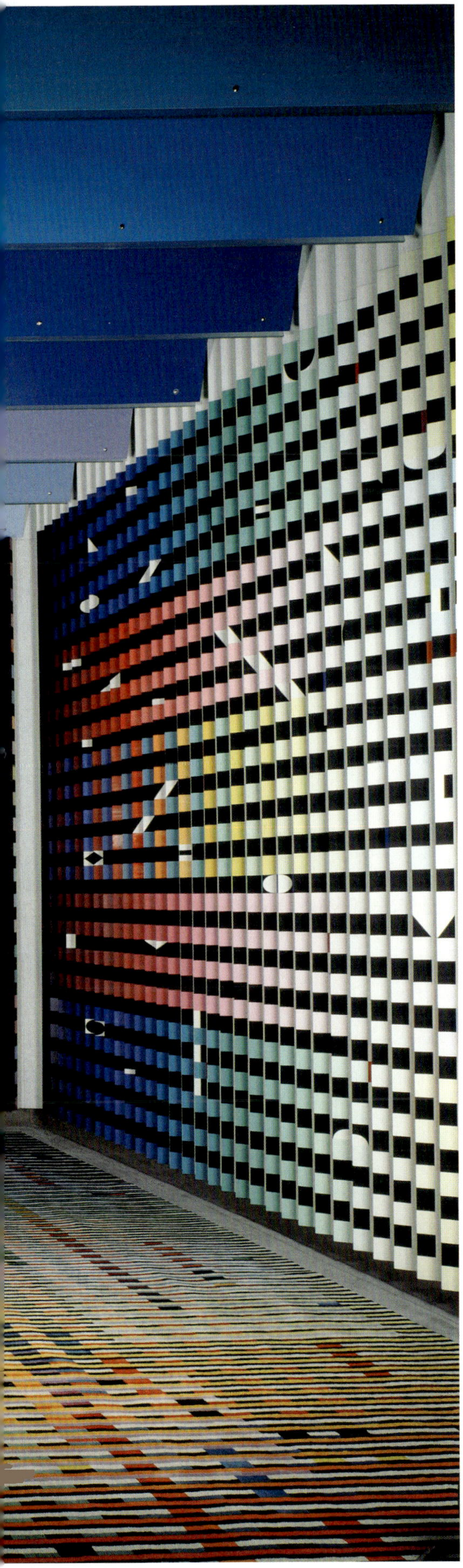

though the Napoleonic armchairs were removed from sight). Cabinet meetings were transferred to the Murat Room, a tradition that almost seemed perpetual.

Pompidou's metamorphosis began, in an experimental way, in the private apartments upstairs, where the arrival of chairs by Eero Saarinen and furnishings by François Arnal and Pierre Paulin was met by historic items stamped by Sené and Jacob. Jean Coural of the National Furniture Depository, a great connoisseur of historic furniture and an art historian with a solid classical background, admiringly described the harmony of apartments renovated right down to the service rooms, "which shed their startling collection of cupboards of every shape and style." The Élysée's transformation began gently—largely thanks to Coural—yet resolutely.

First Lady Claude Pompidou oversaw everything—the Mies van der Rohe stool, the Roger Tallon television stand, the Vasarely carpet, an Étienne Hajdu carpet woven in Lodève, and paintings by Jean Fautrier, Max Ernst, and above all Nicolas de Staël (the first artist whose work—a small one—the Pompidous had bought for themselves years earlier). In the ground-floor reception rooms, however, the main effort was to replace the Empire style (except in the Silver Room, from which a freakish Empire-Poincaré desk was removed) by an appropriately eighteenth-century look, employing the finest items in the Furniture Depository. The Pompidou style had its own, fully acknowledged, Pompadour touch.

LEFT The op-art décor of the antechamber to the private apartments of President and Madame Pompidou, commissioned from Yaacov Agam in 1971, was installed in the Élysée by the National Furniture Depository in 1972–74. By covering walls, ceiling, floor, and doors in op art, the concept of "polymorphic" painting (which changed as viewpoint changed) was elevated to the level of interior design. The installation is now conserved in the National Museum of Modern Art in the Pompidou Center.
BELOW President and Madame Pompidou also liked historic interiors. Here they are seen in the Silver Room, June 21, 1969.

More spectacular were the changes that began in 1971 in the private sector of the reception wing. There survive a kitchen with resin paneling and a huge light fixture of luminous rods hanging from twenty-two coffers in the ceiling, a bathroom, and a small dressing room decorated by Paulin. The Pompidous turned to the Atelier de Recherche et de Création, a creative workshop within the Furniture Depository, which they visited in October 1969. And they adopted the principle of thorough yet reversible redecoration. An antechamber designed by Yaacov Agam, an artist discovered at the Denise René Gallery, was a total environment (and is now an artwork in the National Museum of Modern Art in the Pompidou Center). Op art reigned, making viewers blink as their vision altered—the space was transformed with every new step, every new moment (conveying a whole political and philosophical message). Perhaps for the first time since Madame de Pompadour and the Auriol presidency, the Élysée became a testing ground for some of the boldest stylistic initiatives of the day. Following Agam's visual shock, the drawing room, smoking room, and dining room decorated by Paulin were conducive to the hanging of paintings by the likes of Frantisek Kupka and Robert Delaunay, abolishing the line between walls and furniture, just as the old woodwork had done when married to armchairs and sofas.

Yet how many people realized that these novelties represented a return to the spirit of the eighteenth century, to a similar inspiration? President Pompidou suggested as much to savvy visitors by having Boucher's portrait of Madame de Pompadour placed here on an easel: the painting wasn't anachronistic, but rather synchronic. There then arose the opportunity to relieve the Ballroom of its decorum, which would have been a courageous act, for it meant revamping a ceremonious site associated with de Gaulle. But Pompidou died in office before work could begin.

The ever-practical Giscard d'Estaing used the central office only for ceremonial meetings—he worked in a lighter, more pleasant corner room, fitted out with rare furniture that he simultaneously desanctified and resanctified by littering them with personal photos, souvenirs, and books. His successors have done the same, thereby domesticating the residence where, Giscard admitted, de Gaulle had intimidated him. The presidential Library recovered its former appearance, but Giscard replaced the Elysian background with a French flag when he posed there for Jacques Henri Lartigue, a photographer associated with the elegant lifestyle of the 1930s.

Loyal to Louis XV but attracted to the purity of the Louis-XVI style, Giscard was interested in the latter period and brought some fine furnishings into the Élysée, without seeking to reconstruct an implausible period setting. A small rug beneath his desk protected the large, costly carpet, especially when his dog Jugurtha showed up. Giscard favored a different view of the Élysée, punctuating a tour with a few depictions of famous guests: he placed a portrait of Louis XV after Van Loo on the central mirror of the Ambassadors Room, a portrait of Napoleon when still first consul (a recent copy, from Malmaison, of the famous portrait by Ingres, now in Liège), and one of Princess Mathilde in court dress by Édouard Dubufe (father of Guillaume Dubufe, who painted the ceiling of the Ballroom), as though the residence had sailed harmoniously through every governmental regime, a kind of family home for the French.

The nearby rooms were relieved of their reversible décors by Agam and Paulin, but the kitchen remained unchanged and was used by Giscard, a sign that he was perhaps seeking a balance rather than being completely anti-modernist.

ABOVE *Study for the Private Apartments in the Élysée: Perspective View of Dressing Room* by Pierre Paulin, gouache, 1971 (Musée National d'Art Moderne, Centre Pompidou Paris.)

FACING PAGE The dining room decorated by Pierre Paulin, with the cocktail bar by François-Xavier and Claude Lalanne that features facing ostriches made by the Sèvres porcelain manufactory. President Pompidou and his wife transformed the first four rooms of the east wing into a modern apartment that gave free rein to contemporary French design.

ABOVE AND RIGHT The screening room in the basement. The hallway and staircase leading there are adorned with posters of famous movies such as *Le Président*, starring Jean Gabin, directed by Henri Verneuil.

The renovation of the Ballroom was postponed once again (and anyway, in 1972 the interior of the Train Bleu restaurant in the Gare de Lyon was listed as an historic monument, indicating that the 1900 baroque revival had come back into fashion). More urgent was the installation of an underground command bunker in the former air-raid shelter, as was cleaning the façade and updating the wiring.

During the Mitterrand presidency (1981–95), the private apartments were redone by talented interior decorators Anne Tribel, Marc Held, Ronald Cécil Sportes, Philippe Starck, and Jean-Michel Wilmotte (who did the president's bedroom). But these changes remained little known. Perhaps more attentive to symbols than his predecessors, Mitterrand left his mark on palace history through two moves that were truly striking: at the entrance he placed a sculpted group by Arman, and he ordered new furniture for his office from Paulin, with lamps by Cini Boeri. Paulin had apparently evolved from his style of the Pompidou years, and he added a surprising blue note to the Golden Room. Mitterrand's strong furnishing statement coincided with his election to a second term.

After Mitterrand, French presidents have kept their hands off the symbols of the nation's heritage. The most important changes took place under Nicolas Sarkozy (2007–12), who had the façades, balconies, and floors redone without imposing a personal touch anywhere. This deliberate decision was revealed to defenders of French heritage including Jean-Marie Pérouse de Montclos, invited to view the result of the work during a lunch attended by Sarkozy's minister of culture, Frédéric Mitterrand (nephew of former President Mitterrand). President François Hollande (2012–17), meanwhile, showed little interest in the Élysée, except for turning off the lights in the upstairs office himself every night before leaving, perhaps recalling that de Gaulle had the same habit, which the French view as a sign of greatness.

A Presidential Style?

Philippe Starck knew what he was doing in 2005 when he designed his Louis Ghost chair, a modern equivalent of the Chiararina—a delicate, gilded chair found throughout palatial residences—being a "period" piece of no particular period or style. These days, whose names get linked to a "style"? Designers have replaced aristocrats—there is a now-classic "Paulin style," and there was perhaps an "Auriol style," but it is hard to imagine a "Hollande style" or "Sarkozy style." It is history that assigns names. Nobody referred to a "Charles-X style" in the days of Charles X. Yet Charles Garnier's probably apocryphal reply to Empress Eugénie, who was puzzled at the sight of the new opera house he had just designed—"It's the Napoleon-III style, Madame"—expresses the unavowed ambition of the powerful to leave their name in the "grammar" of styles, thereby becoming a "ghost."

A macho—and Manichean—attitude long assumed that modifications to presidential residences were the work of wives and mistresses. But Giscard d'Estaing was an extraordinary expert on the eighteenth century, and he even published a long article on the French economy under Louis XV in the catalog of an exhibition held at the Mint in Paris in 1974, *The Age of Louis XV: A Moment of Perfection in French Arts* (a title that conveys it all). His wife, Anne-Aymone, shared Giscard's interest and was familiar with the decorative art collections in the Louvre and the Museum of Decorative Arts, but it really can't be said that she left a personal mark on the Élysée. Similarly, the Pompidou couple's enthusiasm for de Staël and Paulin was shared. Their "Agam Room" has now been moved to the museum in the Pompidou Center. There is a logic to conserving a room in a museum: it marks an episode in the history of styles. Changing the name of the Georges Pompidou Center to the Pompidou Center without the first name was a way to acknowledge the shared creativity of Georges and Claude, united in their new vision of a décor minus the decorum—they apparently enjoyed pushing the furniture around at night themselves, to the stupefaction of the palace ushers.

FACING PAGE President Valéry Giscard d'Estaing, in the Golden Room, 1974. The president's taste for the eighteenth century was expressed in the names given to rooms and in his choice of furniture, which sought to impart historical coherence to the palace. A small rug protects the masterful Savonnerie carpet woven for the Louvre Palace under Louis XIV.

RIGHT A room of modernist paintings, designed by Pierre Paulin, in the private apartment of President and Madame Pompidou in the Élysée, July 15, 1974. Two canvases by Frantisek Kupka flank a painting by Robert Delaunay.

PAGES 84-85 In 1986, under President Mitterrand, modern blue furniture designed by Pierre Paulin was installed in the Golden Room of the Élysée. At the end of his second term, Mitterrand restored the room to its previous state: was this an act of subtle tact, or a refusal to allow his successor to inherit his modernity?

The Élysée and the National Furniture Depository

Madame de Pompadour treated her Paris residence as a showcase, furnished not just for comfort but to demonstrate her support for the finest artisans and luxury-goods dealers as well as the craft manufactories founded by Louis XIV. Her brother, the marquis of Marigny, was director of Royal Works, which meant he oversaw the bustling tapestry workshops of Savonnerie and Gobelins ("one of the finest establishments in France"). In a way, this period gave birth to a natural link between the future presidential palace and what would be called the Mobilier National (National Furniture Depository), heir to the former Royal Wardrobe and all the royal tapestry and furniture workshops. The Pompadour-Marigny period was characterized by constant inventiveness and the involvement of great artists, something that all directors of the National Furniture Depository—from Jean Coural to Jean-Pierre Samoyault and Hervé Lemoine—have obviously kept in mind, thinking foremost of the Élysée, that leading icon. Already, in the interwar period, national workshops were involved in the restoration and embellishment of "the Château," as the Élysée is dubbed. This trend was given greater thrust in 1964 when André Malraux, the minister of culture, founded a creative workshop called the Atelier de Recherche et Création (ARC), designed to impart new impetus to the decorative arts in France. The Élysée has always been a sign of excellence of the "craft trades," even before they were called that, starting with the grand furniture-makers of the eighteenth century. For example, in 1926 the Élysée took delivery of a sideboard designed by Jacques Émile Ruhlmann, featuring amboyna burl marquetry inlaid with ivory, which had been exhibited at the Salon d'Automne in Paris in 1920 as well as in a show of French art held in San Francisco in 1924, and again at the Paris Art Deco Exhibition of 1925. During the presidency of Vincent Auriol (1947–54), furniture by André Arbus was installed upstairs, while furnishings by Louis Süe and Jean-Charles Moreux completed the interior decoration of a bedroom theoretically reserved for foreign

LEFT The dining room used by President and Madame Vincent Auriol (1947–54), as redesigned by Jules Leleu with ceramic furnishings by Luc Lanel in a fleeting demonstration of modern taste within the Élysée. Like the great ocean liners of the day, the postwar presidential palace was expected to flaunt creative French design. These bold moves were soon abandoned, only to recur in a different form under Georges Pompidou (1969–74) and, in smaller touches, François Mitterrand (1981–95), leading to today's furnishings.
FACING PAGE, TOP A sideboard by Jacques Émile Ruhlmann, delivered to the Élysée in 1926. Made for the National Furniture Depository, this masterpiece features amboyna burl marquetry inlaid with ivory. It is decorated with an octagonal plaque of silver-plated bronze by sculptor Simon Foucault, with allegorical figures of Day and Night.
FACING PAGE, BOTTOM A preparatory drawing for Ruhlmann's sideboard (Boulogne-Billancourt, musée des Années Trente, archives Ruhlmann). The mesh-like inlay of ivory is a typical feature of his designs.

monarchs, which de Gaulle found amusing (and thus eliminated, saying he had no desire to bump into a king in pajamas). Although the Auriols' short-lived plan to hire artist Henri Matisse—who would have decorated a reception room based on two tapestries from his own *Polynesia* series, woven at the Beauvais manufactory at that time—never came to fruition, a magnificent dining room by Jules Leleu was briefly installed upstairs; as seen in surviving photos, it had ceramic door- and window-frames, a modern fireplace, and table and chairs that matched a new tapestry woven at Aubusson. It gave that part of the Élysée the look of an ocean liner in the days when those floating palaces were also showcases for young designers whom France wished to promote. Jacqueline Auriol, the president's daughter-in-law, was a pioneering aviator and popular figure who contributed to this enthusiasm for youth and elegance. André Arbus and Louis Süe designed a ceremonial neckchain for the Grand Master of the Order of the Legion of Honor, made by Raymond Subes in 1953, which President Pompidou wore in his official portrait in a subtle sign of this new artistic impetus.

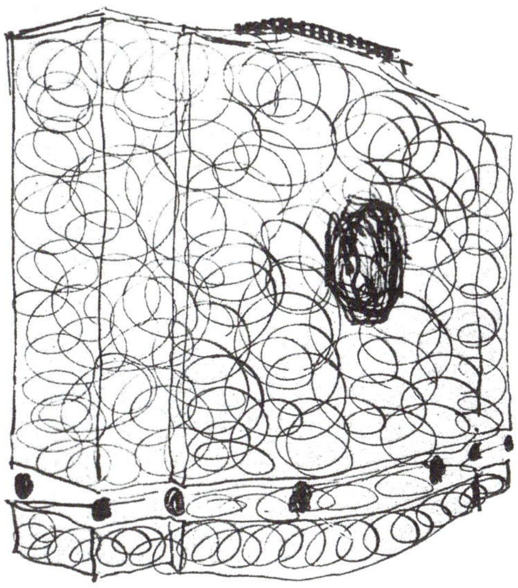

Pompidou's innovations remain famous—when he saw the plans for what would later be called the Pompidou Center he notoriously quipped with delight: "That'll make 'em holler!" His innovations perpetuated the transmission of skills along with a certain idea of French modernism, something still very alive today. A revival style—a desire to reconstitute a former state—is a special taste in itself, one held by Valéry Giscard d'Estaing, who had fine eighteenth-century furniture installed in the Élysée. There was nothing outmoded about Giscard; he also had an "ultra-modern" screening room set up, with armchairs worthy of a palatial movie theater. Nowadays, the hall and stairway to the screening room are decorated with posters that obviously include *Le Président* starring Jean Gabin and *All the President's Men* with Robert Redford and Dustin Hoffmann, as well as *La Grande Vadrouille* and *Of Gods and Men*, directed by Xavier Beauvois.

FACING PAGE Restorers at work on chairs for the Élysée. The National Furniture Depository has seven restoration workshops that perpetuate the peerless quality of French decorative skills.
ABOVE Heir to the Office of the Royal Wardrobe, the National Furniture Depository is charged with conserving heritage furniture as well as with furnishing presidential residences. On the floor level are two Empire-period beds used by Caroline Murat in the Élysée Palace.
RIGHT Furniture for the Silver Room being re-upholstered in lilac silk faille with silver binding.
PAGES 90–91 Artist Évariste Richer recomposed the floor plan of the palace in his Élysée Blue service, a dinner set made by the Sèvres porcelain manufactory in 2018. Richer worked from a 1913 plan, playing on the "blue" code of architectural blueprints in a way that enhances the chefs' own artworks. Designed for three hundred guests, the service includes nine hundred main plates and three hundred side plates.

The Pompadour Spirit and the Myth of an "Original State"

Renovation work begun in 2018 restored the light, cool feel of the pale, eighteenth-century woodwork in the Aides-de-Camp Room, which had been heavily gilded in the nineteenth century to give the residence a "palatial" air to rival the Tuileries Palace. The renovation does not, however, represent a quest for an "original state"—the earlier colors are so suited to modern artworks that some visitors think the walls have been deliberately "lightened" to provide a setting for furnishings by young designers. It is perhaps in this room, where work began, that we can best understand the recent approach. A "Pompadour state," furnished with items that may have been there at the time, would have been a complete fiction, like a set for a costume drama. While most of the woodwork is original, renovations carried out during the Second-Empire (1852–70) added elements that had to be merged with the dominant, eighteenth-century feel.

Work therefore had to advance on two fronts: recover an earlier state of the premises as best as possible, selecting the one that seemed most coherent and best documented (rather than inventing an interior décor, as was previously done); and then furnish it with modern designs. In a way, this approach perpetuates the spirit of the early owners of the mansion in the eighteenth century, thereby restoring the original spirit rather than an appearance that could never be truly authentic.

It also represents a modern assertion of the National Furniture Depository's attachment to "France's leading residence." The Furniture Depository is the official supplier of furnishings, even modest ones, to all "national palaces"—it boasts a unique collection of historic furniture, worthy of the finest museums, which it is responsible for conserving and maintaining. The first crucial, and urgent, task was to send back to the Depository's workshops and warehouses the many furnishings whose basic state of conservation was uncertain. No tapestry remains intact after being hung for nearly a century—threads break, colors fade. Some of the tapestries at the Élysée had become so famous that no one dared touch them. Several Gobelins tapestries had hung in the Ballroom for decades, while *The Expulsion of Heliodorus from the Temple,* woven in 1738 after Raphael's famous fresco, and hanging at the end wall of the Winter Garden, was begging for mercy. Meanwhile, the carpet in the presidential office—the seventieth of a set of ninety-three carpets ordered by Louis XIV for the long riverside gallery in the Louvre (hence a miraculous survivor that has figured in the Crown inventories since 1697 and featured in countless photos since de Gaulle's presidency)—was in danger of irreparable damage if left underfoot. It therefore seemed wiser to replace it with a carpet designed in 1979 by Victor Vasarely, titled *Dark Composition*, which adds a musical note to the painted woodwork and gilded panels. In fact, this refined interior never really accorded with the "historic" Louis-XIV carpet, which was overly royal—the walls dated from the Second Empire and reflected Empress Eugénie's affection for a reinvented eighteenth-century style, in a room that, while magnificent, had no official function. In de Gaulle's day it was thought that the royal carpet matched the gilded walls, thereby combining to create a temple of grandeur and glory. However appealing, this interpretation was misleading; the glitter of the "Golden Room" was originally designed to be festive and youthful with lively, colorful swirls (Napoleon III used it as his music room). Hence it was nonsense to ossify this room—endowed in 1897 with magnificent locks bearing republican emblems—into an "office of the president of the French Republic." France has no need of the fiction of an American-style Oval Office. The new, twenty-first-century version is the product of a convincing approach that stems from the mansion's complicated history, not only conserving and restoring

FACING PAGE Photographed here in the Portrait Room in July 1973, President Pompidou worked on a Gaudreau-stamped desk traditionally used by prime ministers in the Matignon Palace. The large carpet was originally woven for the Tuileries Palace bedroom of the Duke of Angoulême (then heir to the throne). It became so worn from constant visitors that it has now been withdrawn from use, like most of the historic carpets in the Élysée.

heritage features but also conveying the spirit and flavor of the place. More than any other French edifice, the Élysée can continue to promote artisans who pass on peerless skills from generation to generation, thereby preserving an "intangible heritage," as mirrored in the newly gilded woodwork in the Portrait Room, an example of unmatched virtuosity. Restorers of masterpieces and creators of new designs work hand in hand. What does Pierre Soulages think of his painting hung against the paneling of the Golden Room? Does it seem antithetical to him? When shown a photo of an initial attempt to hang it in the Tapestries Room, he pointed out that the painting was not the right way up—a mistake that was immediately corrected. We tend to forget that, ever since he was a boy, Soulages has loved Watteau's paintings, notably the blue light-chiseled sky in *The Embarcation for the Isle of Cythera*.

To what state should the Portrait Room be restored? In Madame de Pompadour's day, the portraits of ancestors over the doors of what had been the Count of Évreux's "drawing room" were symbolically replaced by the classical muses. Although it retains almost all its original woodwork, there was no question of returning this room to its elusive "historic" state. Its constantly changing decoration makes it fascinating. During the Second Empire (1852–70), the room was given a European feel when Napoleon III partly recomposed the setting by replacing the nine muses with eight portraits: Pope Pius IX (on an equal footing with the others), Emperor Franz-Joseph of Austria, King Victor Emmanuel II of Italy, Czar Nicolas I of Russia, Queen Victoria of England, King Frederick-William of Prussia, Queen Isabella II of Spain, and King William I of Wurtemberg (all of whom TV pundits are still able to identify whenever this room is shown on television). It is now used mainly as the president's dining room, after having been the cabinet meeting room during the Third Republic (1870–1940). Its role has changed as often as its historic decoration—the overdoors are witness to the constant swings of French history, having hosted portraits of the imperial family when Caroline and Joachim Murat—Napoleon I's sister and brother-in-law—lived in the mansion. Napoleon III vainly tried to recover those portraits, then came up with the other idea of a concert of nations expressing admiration for France.

FACING PAGE A view of the Portrait Room, restored in autumn 2019. The black vase on the mantelpiece, designed by Pierre Soulages and made by the Sèvres porcelain manufactory in 2000, is the artist's only foray into the realm of pottery.

MEANWHILE, IN THE OFFICES...

The offices on the attic floor and in the wings are full of surprises. Ever since the maze of small offices has encroached on what were the private apartments in the days of Jacques and Bernadette Chirac (1995–2007), some advisers work alongside bathtubs surviving from former bathrooms designed by Alberto Pinto.

Not many presidential advisers bother with decoration. Most simply hang the usual engraved prints from the Louvre showing lavish royal celebrations under Louis XIV—an ironic commentary on their own studious work, which can either come to a sudden end or last for years in these imitation settings. Sometimes the corridors still display artworks that arrived at the Élysée during previous terms of office: "That's not water damage from a leak," goes an often-heard joke, "that's a loan from the National Museum of Modern Art." These poor souls, who never actually see what commentators inevitably refer to as "the nation's gilded palaces," fill their offices with books they don't have the time to read (thereby becoming a kind of talisman) or music they don't dare play too loudly. A stairway leads directly to the waiting room downstairs and, from there, across the Green Room to the president's office. It's one of the busiest paths of everyday traffic at "the château."

There is a stark contrast between the serene silence of the ground-floor reception rooms and the bustle of the offices in the side wings. The contrast is even starker underground, in the basement passages (used for crossing the courtyard without getting buttonholed by busybodies) and in the kitchens with their constant to-and-fro. Considered "show kitchens" ever since they were installed in the basement of the west end—back in the days of President Auriol (1947–54)—they boast some relics like copper pans bearing the stamp of the Tuileries

LEFT At the top of the main staircase an usher still greets the president's guests, but Jean Olivier Hucleux's portrait of François Mitterrand and the other paintings that formerly comprised a small gallery of presidents are no longer there to intimidate visitors with their unflinching gazes.
FACING PAGE Ushers prepare the next cabinet meeting in the Murat Room. A famous twin-dial clock by Lepaute, placed in the middle of the table, allows the president and the prime minister, who sit opposite each other, to see the time.

Palace and ovens worthy of an old ocean liner, yet are too far from the rooms where lunches and dinners are served. Bernadette Chirac personally oversaw the bustling staff in their aprons and white gloves, who work hard to maintain France's reputation. Tall cupboards hold dishes and cutlery that tell their own stories of commissions from porcelain and silver manufactories in an unbroken artistic and craft tradition dating back to the ancien régime—testament to the savoir-faire that is perhaps France's most successful export.

Up until President Hollande's term (2012–17), rooms on the corner of the Rue du Faubourg Saint-Honoré and Avenue de Marigny housed the "duty apartment" where, in rotation, the president's closest advisers would be on night duty. It had its advantages, notably the minor privilege—abolished once the apartment was divided into two—of being able to host a "duty" dinner that could employ the resources of the palace kitchens. These friendly meals were an opportunity to bring journalists, writers, and friends together. Advisers outdid themselves in cultivating contacts, so that an editor of the Pléiade edition of Balzac might meet a fashion designer, or a legendary explorer (and friend of Jacques Chirac) could recount his exploits to amazed inspectors of finance. Perhaps the advisers' "informal" dinners were discontinued precisely because they were more brilliant and fun than official parties.

FACING PAGE AND ABOVE Alma Palace—located between the Eiffel Tower and the new Quai Branly Museum—was built in 1861–64 to house the imperial stables. The vast complex, organized around a main courtyard, included a riding ring, storerooms, housing, and a residential lodge; the stables were divided into two distinct parts, one for horses on the left and another for carriages—including the postal service—on the right.
RIGHT In August 1881, a law conferred use of Alma Palace on the presidential administration, designed to house stables for the head of state. Listed as a historic monument 2002, the complex has recently been restored and is now used by various departments of the president's office.

ON THE GROUNDS OF THE ÉLYSÉE

In the days when a garden party was held on the grounds of the Élysée every July 14—Bastille Day—the lawn would become a swamp if it rained, at which point old army officers would refer to "the quagmire of Dien Bien Phu," while the gardeners claimed it would take a year for the lawn to recover. Since this huge party has not been held since 2010, the grounds have recovered their charm, along with their mystery.

The palace grounds can barely be glimpsed when the back gate opens to allow passage of a presidential motorcade (as it did to allow Parisians to cheer President Faure in his lavish four-horse carriage). In fact, the grounds are a palimpsest, a green sheet of parchment to be read like a medieval manuscript that has been scraped clean and written over, several times. The garden's various incarnations present a dendrochronology of the French Republic. The grounds, like the interior of the palace itself, are haunted by memories of things past: maybe some of the trees are the ones climbed by President Paul Deschanel during his brief term (1920) before he was led away to an asylum? Is the reflecting pool really the one where Vincent Auriol (1947–54) complained he was obliged to "keep going in circles?"

The grounds were the site of an imaginary contest between Presidents Giscard d'Estaing and Mitterrand. Toward the end of his first term, the former, confident of re-election, began redesigning the garden. A row of some thirty linden trees was planted parallel to Avenue de Marigny, pruned into a screen—this was the start of a Pompadour-revival scheme that matched the redecoration of the interior. It was designed to recreate the harmony of a French formal garden based on eighteenth-century plans. Behind the still-windowless Ballroom Giscard had envisaged a gravel-paved "green room," namely a semicircular curtain of yew trees that would form a kind of verdant theater, in the most recent act of the Versailles revival that periodically graces the arts in France.

Planted in front of the side wing were boxwood hedges in elaborate, Louis-XV-style patterns, designed by an architect from the Monuments Historiques who in fact simply modified a 1913 layout from Madame de Poincaré's rose garden. When Danielle Mitterrand became First Lady, the pattern was altered by Jacques Wirtz, who also designed the Carrousel Garden in the Tuileries. A perfect palimpsest: at this very spot there has always been a "small flower garden," seen on Mollet's initial plan for the Count of Évreux, even before the days of Madame de Pompadour. The one that survives today is different, but serves the same purpose, because in the meantime an artistic landscaper, Louis Benech, magnificently enriched the composition under the supervision of Bernadette Chirac. Gardeners still refer to the "rose garden" today even though it has no roses (the same syndrome as the Cleopatra Room indoors). Usage and terrain have their laws: flowers are kept close to the house for composing bouquets, while the large, valley-like lawn is a vestige of late eighteenth-century transformations, when trees were already growing along the edge of the plot despite the embankments and the creation of modest terraces. Indeed, the plot existed prior to the residence—as mentioned above, it had been a nursery that André Le Nôtre inherited from his father. The soil was originally very damp, but with all the surrounding construction the water table along the Champs-Élysées has

FACING PAGE The skillful disorder of the garden and its screens of foliage with their gaps and transparencies. A hint of the city is just beyond the grated fence.

dropped forty feet; the first pond dried and stagnated, bringing mosquitoes, and thus had to be eliminated. Yet the transformation into a landscape garden hadn't changed the basic distribution of masses, so the return to a previous state might have been possible and maybe even successful. Giscard, however, failed to complete this project, having lost the election.

Every president likes his garden, inevitably enjoyed with his dog, from Giscard's Jugurtha to Emmanuel Macron's Nemo. In Mitterrand's day, during the reign of his Labrador, Baltique, a study was undertaken by the national landscape school in Versailles, with Gilles Clément providing the ideas and Jacques Wirtz reinstalling three water features that created a vista with a focal point (including fountain spray visible from the exterior). The view was finest from the windows of the Golden Room. The Grand Palais in the background might have been a Crystal Palace at the end of the garden. A little cascade—a reduced-scale, modern version of the "Ballroom Grove" at Versailles—provided a water feature at the end of the Ballroom. Under Mitterrand, Wirtz also added a small garden with vegetation that reminded the president of his country home in the Landes region of southwest France—covered with heath-peat, it was used as an outdoor office. And, although subsequently paved, it is still used as such—discussions are held there when discretion is essential (it is alleged that unacknowledged participants sometimes enter the grounds by a back entrance). Under President Chirac, Louis Benech made it easier to maintain the garden by planting hardy perennials and installing a small greenhouse—symmetrically copying the roof of the Marigny Theater—specifically designed to house all those poor orchids so often offered as a gift to the president.

Two plane trees are the oldest in the garden—two hundred and thirty or maybe even two hundred and fifty years old. Every president wants to leave his mark on these rarely seen grounds, which even the dogs find gloomy. Ultimately, successive terms have brought only modest changes to the sober lawn with its *ostinato rigore* (relentless rigor), while the two plane trees—probably the oldest now dominating Paris skies—seem to mock the head of state: "Everything on earth belongs to princes," wrote Victor Hugo in his poem *La Rose de l'Infante*, "except the wind."

FACING PAGE, TOP *The Mayors of France Being Received on the Grounds of the Élysée Palace* by Fernand Cormon, oil on canvas, 1904 (Châteaux de Versailles et de Trianon). On September 22, 1900, for the International Exposition being held in Paris, President Émile Loubet hosted 22,965 mayors and local officials. The banquet that followed remains the largest seated meal in French history.
FACING PAGE, BOTTOM A garden party on July 14–Bastille Day–during the presidency of Valéry Giscard d'Estaing (1973–81). After the annual military parade, a reception on the grounds of the Élysée hosted several thousand guests, a tradition that continued up to 2010.
RIGHT President Mitterrand and his Labrador on the grounds of the Élysée, 1981. Photo by Gisèle Freund (L'Institut Mémoires de l'Édition Contemporaine, Saint-Germain-la-Blanche-Herbe).
FAR RIGHT President Macron and his Labrador, Nemo. Photo by Soazig de La Moissonnière.

FROM THE OTHER SIDE OF THE STREET

The Élysée has burst its seams. On the Rue de l'Élysée side, buildings have steadily been purchased by the presidential administration—the office of the adviser on African affairs has a pretty terrace, while a well-designed press room has been installed at number 4. On the other side, the Marigny mansion across the street has become an annex of the palace; long used to house official guests, it is now employed for meetings and offices of the departments the president wishes to keep close by.

Several buildings once occupied the plot where the Rue de Élysée was cut. The largest was a mansion facing Avenue Gabriel, bought in 1784 by François-Xavier de Saxe, thus called the "Saxe mansion." Its grandeur appealed to a subsequent buyer, Horace Sébastiani (a general and diplomat under his fellow Corsican, Napoleon I, later named a marshal under King Louis-Philippe, and several times caricatured by Honoré Daumier). In this house Sébastiani's daughter was killed by her husband, the Duke of Praslin, in one of the scandals leading to the Revolution of 1848. The accursed mansion, bought by the Duke of Galliera, was demolished during the Second Empire when Napoleon III decided to protect the Élysée by creating an elegant new style of residential street, called Avenue de la Reine-Hortense (now Rue de Élysée). Émile Pereire designed the development to feature English-style houses with front steps; on the corner, however, Empress Eugénie had architect Hector Martin Lefuel build her a mansion. In 1873 Baron Maurice de Hirsch, a businessman and philanthropist, moved into the mansion and redecorated it; the magnificent staircase, lavish reception rooms, and garden all survive. The premises were acquired for the French presidency in 1967 with the idea of demonstrating the importance the country paid to the new cabinet for African and Madagascan Affairs, which first moved in there.

The adjacent residence, also owned by the extremely wealthy Baron Hirsch, was purchased by the government in 1984. As early as 1960 the Élysée had bought, in this same street, the house occupied by the great art collector Maurice Fenaille. An enlightened patron and friend of Rodin, Fenaille was a member of the Academy of Fine Arts and bequeathed his château in Montal to the nation, as well as enabling the Friends of the Louvre to give *The Turkish Bath* by Ingres to the museum. As a great connoisseur of tapestries, notably those woven at Gobelins, Fenaille advised the Gobelins manufactory on the patterns for the ones it supplied when the Élysée's Ballroom was renovated in 1932. Thus under de Gaulle the presidential staff headquarters and postal service could move into the Fenaille house. The palace complex also includes other houses on this pretty street, which have now been restored (revealing, behind the partition walls and false ceilings in one of them, a bijou little Second-Empire theater).

BELOW The Rue de l'Élysée (then named Avenue de la Reine-Hortense) was laid out with English-style houses during the Second Empire (1852–70).
FACING PAGE The English-style houses on Rue de l'Élysée are an example of experimental urban development: these elegant, modern town houses were highly sought-after under Napoleon III (1852–70), and today almost all of them have become annexes of the presidential palace—one currently hosts the press room.

THE MARIGNY MANSION

The mansion at 23 Avenue de Marigny has a powerful personality. In 1872, Gustave de Rothschild, who had bought two residences, on Avenue de Marigny and Rue du Cirque, asked his favorite architect, Alfred Philibert Aldrophe (who designed the synagogue on Rue de la Victoire), to combine them, transforming them into a majestic edifice designed first and foremost for receptions. The resulting early Third-Republic architecture represents the final throes of an eclecticism on its death bed. One big problem concerned the difference in ground levels. Once past the front gate, the courtyard (which retained part of the original glass house that, during evening parties, would light up like an enchanted crystal palace), and then the round entrance hall, you had to climb a circular staircase on the left to finally reach a so-called ground floor with reception rooms—an intriguing surprise that startled visitors. This arrangement meant that the domestic services could be lodged in the basement level.

That may be why the most impressive room is the entrance hall with its magnificent lantern, which established a link between the courtyard façade, where portions of the former Choiseul mansion were reinstalled like ornaments, and the façade on the garden side, of eighteenth-century inspiration.

No one realized that this superlative piece of architecture—a collage of quotations of ancient features, as well as a joint tribute to the grand stables at Chantilly and the finest aristocratic town houses in Enlightenment Paris—contained a hidden treasure. What everyone thought was a garden seat decorated with griffins (behind which watering cans were stored), turned out to be by far the oldest item in the collection of the French presidential administration, namely a capital from the temple of Apollo at Didyma, an archaeological site in Asia Minor whose excavation was financed by Gustave and Edmond de Rothschild. In 1873 the brothers presented the Louvre with a magnificent set of sculptures, yet held on to this modest fragment as a talisman, which was swiftly forgotten (but is now in the Louvre).

The Rothschild style, inevitably associated with enlightened collecting and support for French museums, is visible in the Marigny mansion. Starting in 1876, commissions went to artists such as Henri Lévy and Eugène Lami—the latter decorated princely interiors like the private apartments of the Duke and Duchess of Aumale as well as the Grand Hall of the Château of Ferrières for the Rothschilds themselves. Overdoors by Paul Baudry (one of the artists on Charles Garnier's team at the new Opéra), originally from an old town house, were installed; bronze vases adorned with putti (based on models at Versailles) were placed on stone plinths lining the large flower beds in the garden, for which marble sphinxes were carved. The room today lined in theatrical golden yellow silk served as a setting for venerable items such as carved doors from the Château of Bastie d'Urfé, bought in 1889 (and returned there in 1975, now replaced by copies); the ceiling painted by Lami offers a foretaste of the rest of the visit. In the large, Versailles-revival reception rooms, a tapestry with the coat of arms of France is hung between red-marble pilasters; next door, Louis-XV-revival woodwork creates a setting for a tapestry woven to cartoons by Pierre Victor Galland, who painted the ceiling of the Music Room in the

FACING PAGE Visitors to the Marigny mansion are struck by the magnificent lantern in the entrance hall; arriving from the street, they climb a staircase that leads, on the left to the main building overlooking the garden.
PAGES 108-9 This urban mansion is a triumph of the lavish and eclectic "Rothschild style," characterized by historical allusions and the re-use of woodwork and paintings that dialogue with more modern commissions.

Jacquemart-André mansion (now museum). Today these splendors create an unusual context for meetings in which "theater of operations" has replaced festive theatricals, and where the wording of draft agreements has replaced readings of the eighteenth-century pastoral novel *L'Astrée* by Honoré d'Urfé. A few watercolors by Alexandre Serebriakoff (a "portraitist of interiors" during the final glow of the Café Society) make it possible to imagine the Marigny mansion still alive to the rhythm of high-society entertainment.

Robert de Rothschild, who inherited this composite, extravagant property in 1912, had Jean-Charles Moreux design new gardens in 1928, putting a swimming pool and gym in the back of the grounds, as well as a surprising folly decorated with mirrors, and a mural by Giorgio De Chirico (pictures of which were found by historian Pauline Prévost-Marcilhacy in the archives of the Institut Français d'Architecture). By the 1970s the fashion had passed for the Rothschilds' nineteenth-century interiors; the most notorious example, the Château of Ferrières, was donated by the heirs to the University of Paris, while the Marigny mansion was bought by the Office of the President. Today this grand dwelling, which symbolically bears the name of Madame de Pompadour's brother (the Marquis of Marigny), seems to form a link between the Élysée's venerable woodwork and today's styles, a link too little appreciated in the history of taste forged not just by architects and artists but also by artisan carvers and ornamentalists. Albert Cruchet, son of Michel Victor Cruchet (inventor of the *carton-pierre* technique and creator of much woodwork and furnishings for Empress Eugénie), was hired by Gustave de Rothschild to decorate his home and thus deserves mention alongside Aldrophe, as does Jacques Verberckt, who worked with the architect Gabriel for Madame de Pompadour. They are links in a continuous chain, members of the historical line of fine French artisans whose descendents are still at work in Marigny and the Élysée today—perhaps with different ideas and methods, but with the same pride.

LEFT *View of the Garden, Hôtel de Marigny*, watercolor by Alexandre Serebriakoff, 1972 (private collection).
FACING PAGE *The Green Room, Hôtel de Marigny* (detail), watercolor by Alexandre Serebriakoff, 1972 (private collection). The Marigny mansion was home to collectors, and it is still possible to imagine that it once looked a veritable museum.

The Élysée Palace
The Entrance

ABOVE AND FACING PAGE The entrance to the Élysée Palace at 55 Rue du Faubourg Saint-Honoré. The Second-Empire crest has been replaced by symbols of the French Republic.

The Courtyard

FACING PAGE An imperial eagle still lurks beneath the main archway to the Élysée.
ABOVE Grotesque masks adorning the main courtyard.
PAGES 116–17 The courtyard with its classical, very eighteenth-century look was entirely reconstructed under Napoleon III (1852–70).

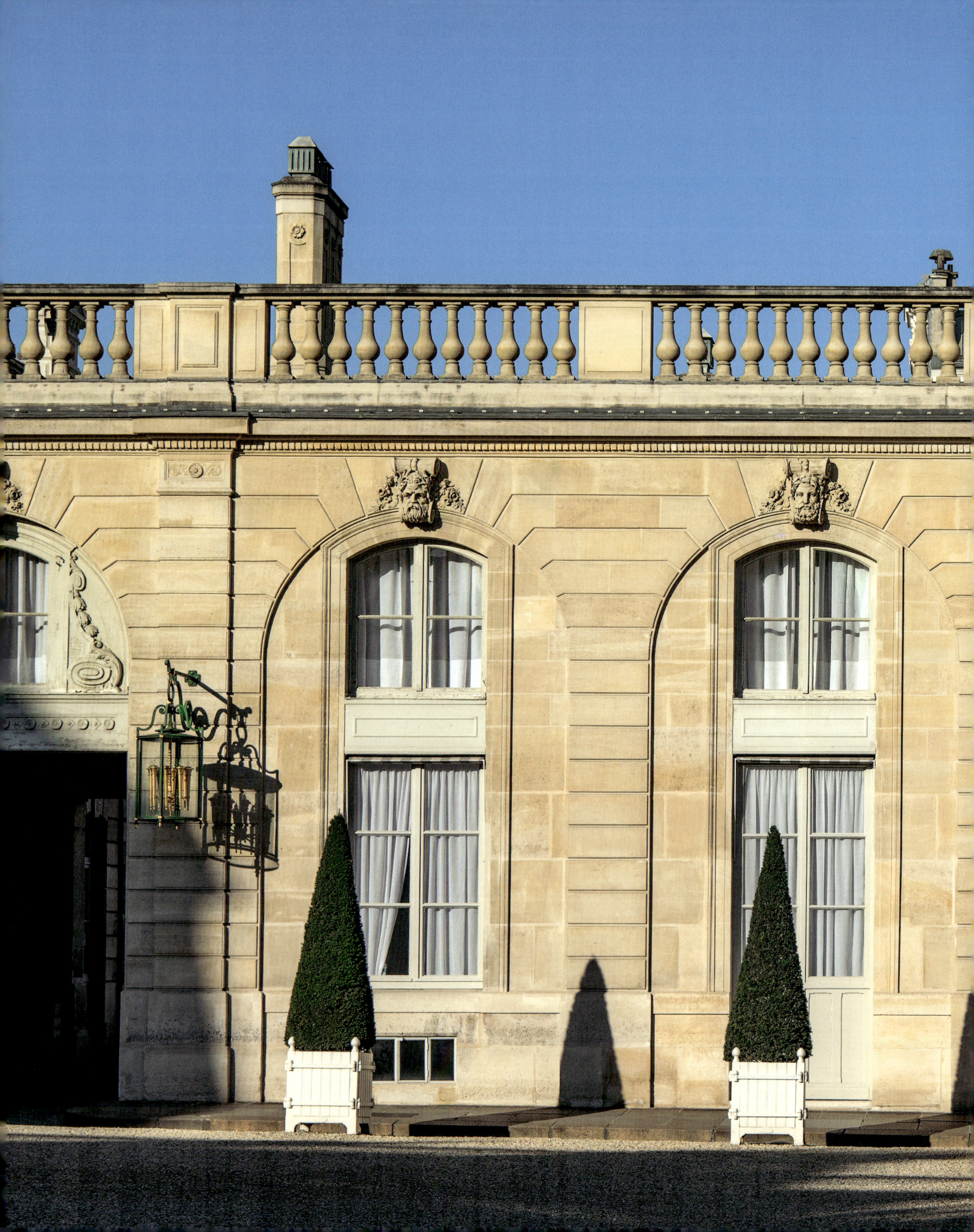

BELOW Even during a Covid pandemic, the Republican Guard continues to greet distinguished visitors on the steps of the porch of the palace.
FACING PAGE The horse heads and oak leaves on the former stables—now used for offices—still evoke their military use.

"Since Versailles would have been excessive, the Trianon was in danger of collapse, Fontainebleau, Rambouillet and Compiègne were too far away, and Vincennes—which I considered—was in [the] process of restoration, I settled for what was immediately available and had, moreover, become adapted to time-honored Parisian administrative habits. The new Republic, then, so far as its functioning and its reputation were concerned, would make the most of the old Élysée."

Charles de Gaulle, *Memoirs of Hope: Renewal, 1958–1962.*

The Entrance Hall

RIGHT Large panes of glass bring transparency to the entrance hall, an idea that dates back to renovations under President Auriol (1947–54).

FACING PAGE The cloakroom on the other side of the staircase is well hidden.
ABOVE In the entrance hall, to the right of the Arman sculpture and the pair of candle stands, hangs *Composition* by Nicolas de Staël (oil on canvas, 1949, Centre Pompidou). Above it, a First-Empire medallion features the prow of a ship, reminding visitors that Marshal Joachim Murat was also an admiral.

The Staircase

BELOW AND FACING PAGE To the left of the entrance hall, the main staircase of limestone has a first flight of twenty-three steps to a landing, from which two more flights lead to the second floor. The banister of upright palm leaves rising from rosettes set within olive wreaths is made of bronze- and gold-plated lead.

The Cleopatra Room

FACING PAGE The Cleopatra Room takes it name from a Gobelins tapestry that no longer hangs there. *Antony Meeting Cleopatra,* woven from a design by Charles Joseph Natoire, was placed there under President Carnot (1887–94), but has now been replaced by a tapestry woven in 2010 from an untitled design by Yves Oppenheim. On the floor is a carpet by Jean-Paul Philippe, *Mnemos Marelle* (Hopscotch Mnemonics, 2001).
BELOW A glass sculpture by Ettore Sottsass, *Lingam* (2001), stands on a Louis-XV commode bearing the stamp of Mathieu Criaerd.

The Ambassadors Room

BELOW AND PAGES 130-31 The Ambassadors Room owes its name to a practice instituted by President MacMahon (1875–79) of having foreign ambassadors present their credentials there. The white marble fireplace—a Second-Empire copy of one in the royal council chamber at Versailles—is embellished with a set of gilt-bronze Louis-XVI candlesticks and andirons.

FACING PAGE Since 2017 the Ambassadors Room has often hosted Wednesday-morning cabinet meetings. Sometimes, as seen here, the table is set for a special lunch with a guest whom the president particularly wishes to honor.

FACING PAGE A table in the Ambassadors Room laid with the Diana service designed by Étienne Hajdu in 1970 for the Sèvres porcelain manufactory. Here Hadju transposed his ink-splash drawings onto porcelain. The tablecloth is the Papyrus design by the D. Porthault firm.
ABOVE Detail of the gilt-bronze mounts on the fireplace in the Ambassadors Room.

The Pompadour Room

FACING PAGE Madame de Pompadour's former "ceremonial bedchamber" retains the two columns flanking the semicircular alcove holding her bed, after which the room was originally named. Rechristened the Pompadour Room, it still has its eighteenth-century woodwork, yet hosts furniture that varies with the tastes of a given occupant. The current furniture consists of a sofa-and-ottoman suite by Thierry Lemaire (Niko, 2019), a low table by Martin Szekely (1980), and a tapestry by Richard Rapaich (Elégia, 1985).

BELOW The overdoor panels painted by Charles Chaplin during the Second Empire shows Roman goddesses Diana, Minerva, Venus, and—seen here—Juno holding a scepter, accompanied by a peacock.

The Portrait Room

ABOVE During the Second Empire (1852–70), ministerial cabinet meetings were held in this room. Napoleon III had it decorated with eight portraits of Europe's leading monarchs.
FACING PAGE Restored in 2019, the Portrait Room triggers a dialogue between eighteenth-century woodwork, nineteenth-century paintings, and twenty-first-century art embodied by the famous black vase by Pierre Soulages. In the mirrors can been seen portraits of Queen Isabella II of Spain and King William I of Wurtemberg.

ABOVE AND FACING PAGE The Portrait Room gives onto the small flower garden. The hues of the carpet, woven to a design by André-Pierre Arnal (*Window on the Floor*, 2015), echo the colorful crystal-like pier table by Hervé van der Straeten (2020).

BELOW Today the room is used for lunches and dinners with the president's close acquaintances.
FACING PAGE A table set with the Élysée Blue service for an official luncheon.

The Map Room

LEFT The Map Room took its name from a set of tapestries that mapped the Forest of Compiègne, which hung here during the Second Empire (1852–70). This is the room decorated by Yaacov Agam in the early 1970s for President Pompidou and his wife. Today it remains a showcase for modern art, with a painting by Victor Vasarely (*Re.Na.II A*, 1968) that harmonizes with a Savonnerie carpet woven to a design by Julien Gardair (*Bleaches*, 2006).

RIGHT *Aware II* by Jean Degottex (oil on canvas, 1961) stands above a Washington pier table designed by Jean-Michel Wilmotte in the 1980s. The furniture is by Thierry Lemaire. Although the Map Room no longer serves the purpose for which it is named, the maps are still there, hidden behind some of the wood paneling.

The Library

BELOW, LEFT This Library is surprising. No one really looks at it or thinks of using it to read. Instead, it is a random collection of books that recount an equally random history. Alongside a copy of the French Constitution (bound in red and lettered *R.F.*, for République Française) there are books considered essential to the country during various presidencies: *Tristan et Iseult* by Béroul, *La Peau de Chagrin* by Balzac, *Poésies* by Mallarmé, and *Les Lettres de mon Moulin* by Alphonse Daudet, all published by the Imprimerie Nationale. There are also classics that suggest what the Library might have held in the nineteenth century, notably Prosper de Barante's history of the dukes of Burgundy and a sweeping multi-volume history of France, begun in 1855. It would be nice to know when a 1956 book on the philosophy of Karl Marx, by Jean-Yves Calvez, was added to the Library. This room was chosen as the setting for their official portraits by Presidents Charles de Gaulle, Georges Pompidou, François Mitterrand—who, after having posed for Gisèle Freund, also recorded major TV interviews here—and Nicolas Sarkozy. The armchair, designed by Christian Ghion in 2013, has a shell made of carbon fiber, representing the first use of this material by the creative workshop within the National Furniture Depository.

BELOW, RIGHT The row of rooms seen through the Library, the Fern Room, and the Map Room.

FACING PAGE Commissioned for their dining room by President and Madame Pompidou, the famous cocktail bar by François-Xavier and Claude Lalanne, made of biscuit porcelain and metal by the Sèvres porcelain manufactory (1967–70), has been moved to the Library. The moveable egg is an ice bucket.

The Dining Room

BELOW Detail of a door handle in the Paulin-designed dining room.
FACING PAGE The dining room designed by Pierre Paulin for President and Madame Pompidou in the early 1970s was lined with tall panels of synthetic resin and fiberglass. The sofa and armchairs were designed by Paulin for their private apartments.
PAGES 150-51 This monumental light fixture looks like a piece of sculpture. Its twenty-two coffers house a grid of nine thousand crystal shafts and beads placed in front of anodized aluminum reflectors in Tyrian rose, so that the whole thing glows.

ABOVE Next to the dining room is a small bathroom designed by Pierre Paulin.
FACING PAGE These photographs from the 1970s show the dining room during the Pompidou presidency. It had two round tables that seated twelve. Paulin designed a table top of smoked Triplex glass placed on a cast aluminum base covered in the dove-gray plastic used for the cabin of Apollo spacecraft. Twenty-four cast-aluminum chairs upholstered in leather or fabric completed the set.

The Silver Room

ABOVE The clock on the mantelpiece, made for this room around 1808, features a silver-plated bronze sculpture by André Antoine Ravrio depicting "the chariot of Faithfulness driven by Cupid." The ancient-style cart with clock dial for a wheel is drawn by a pretty little curly-haired dog.

FACING PAGE This famous room is named after the silver color of decorative gilding in white gold. It is the only room that still retains its original furniture. Delivered by cabinetmaker Jacob Desmalter in 1805–6, the méridienne sofas, lyre-back chairs, and gondole armchairs with carved swans were originally upholstered in dark red silk and silver binding. In 1812 Napoleon ordered that the furniture be re-upholstered in lilac silk taffeta.

FACING PAGE The chairs copy those made around 1804 by Jacob Desmalter from a design by Charles Percier for Empress Joséphine's boudoir at the Château of Saint-Cloud. They have been re-upholstered in lilac silk faille with silver binding.
ABOVE Detail of the paneling in the Silver Room. Left, a carved panel gilded with white gold; right, a panel painted with a winged putto and doves. This delicate décor, has remained intact since the First Empire.

ABOVE The atmosphere of this room evokes Napoleon's abdication—a facsimile of the archive document is often placed on display here.
FACING PAGE This lyre-backed chair is typical of the Empire furniture made by Jacob Desmalter for the Silver Room. The entire suite was restored by the National Furniture Depository.

The Murat Room

In addition to being used for cabinet meetings, this room has been the site of historic events: it served as a polling place during the first French presidential elections in 1848, and it hosted the signing of the Franco-German Treaty of Reconciliation in 1963.

ABOVE The Murat Room retains decorative details from the Second Empire (1852–70), such as overdoors bearing the initials of Napoleon III and Eugénie.
FACING PAGE Three of five large paintings of vistas, commissioned during the First Empire (1804–14) in honor of Marshal Murat, are still in place. Here *Trajan's Column,* painted by Alexandre Hyacinthe Dunouy, served as a model for the column erected in Place Vendome, Paris.

FACING PAGE Alexandre Hyacinthe Dunouy and Carle Vernet, *View of Château de Benrath*, 1807. The pier table is by Hervé van der Straeten (Psychose, 2008).
BELOW The remainder of the library books, some of which arrived during the Restoration (1814–30), are found on low bookshelves in the Murat Room. One wonders whether ministers, waiting for the president to arrive when this room hosts cabinet meetings, notice the volumes on these shelves. They include Buffon's natural history stamped with Napoleon's crest, Raynouard's troubadour poetry in bindings with King Louis-Philippe's monogram, Lamartine's *Voyage en Orient,* French translations of Goethe, and Simon-Pierre Ballanche's study on the "palingensis [i.e., rebirth] of society." Although the Élysée has a full-time archivist, no one has ever seen a librarian on the premises.

BELOW AND FACING PAGE In the Murat Room, a timepiece known as the Three Clocks, made by J. C. Develly and Robin in 1841, sits on a pier table decorated with gilt-bronze mounts and porcelain plaques (after illustrations by Alexandre Evariste Fragonard) from 1821. The armchairs have been re-upholstered by the National Furniture Depository to lend a discreet touch of modernity to the historic furniture. The famous Cressent desk was temporarily housed here during restoration work.

L'AMOUR.

FACING PAGE, RIGHT, AND BELOW This outstanding pier table in the Murat Room features a frieze rail of blue porcelain set with three plaques depicting the major stages of plant life—germinating, flowering, and fructifying—as well as profile medallions of mythological figures.

The Aides-de-Camp Room

PAGES 168–69 The Aides-de-Camp Room has retained its eighteenth-century décor, except for the white marble fireplace (1860) imitating one in Louis XV's bedchamber at Versailles, and for the overdoors commissioned from Charles Landelle in 1859, depicting allegories of The Elements, Peace, and Discord. This room, furnished with a suite by Thierry Lemaire (2018–19) and a carpet woven to a design by Zao Wou-ki (1977), is now used to receive guests.
ABOVE Detail of the wood paneling in the Aides-de-Camp Room, restored to its eighteenth-century state in 2018.
RIGHT The cool, pale tones of the eighteenth-century woodwork harmonize with the overdoors painted by Charles Landelle. Here is depicted an allegory of Fire.

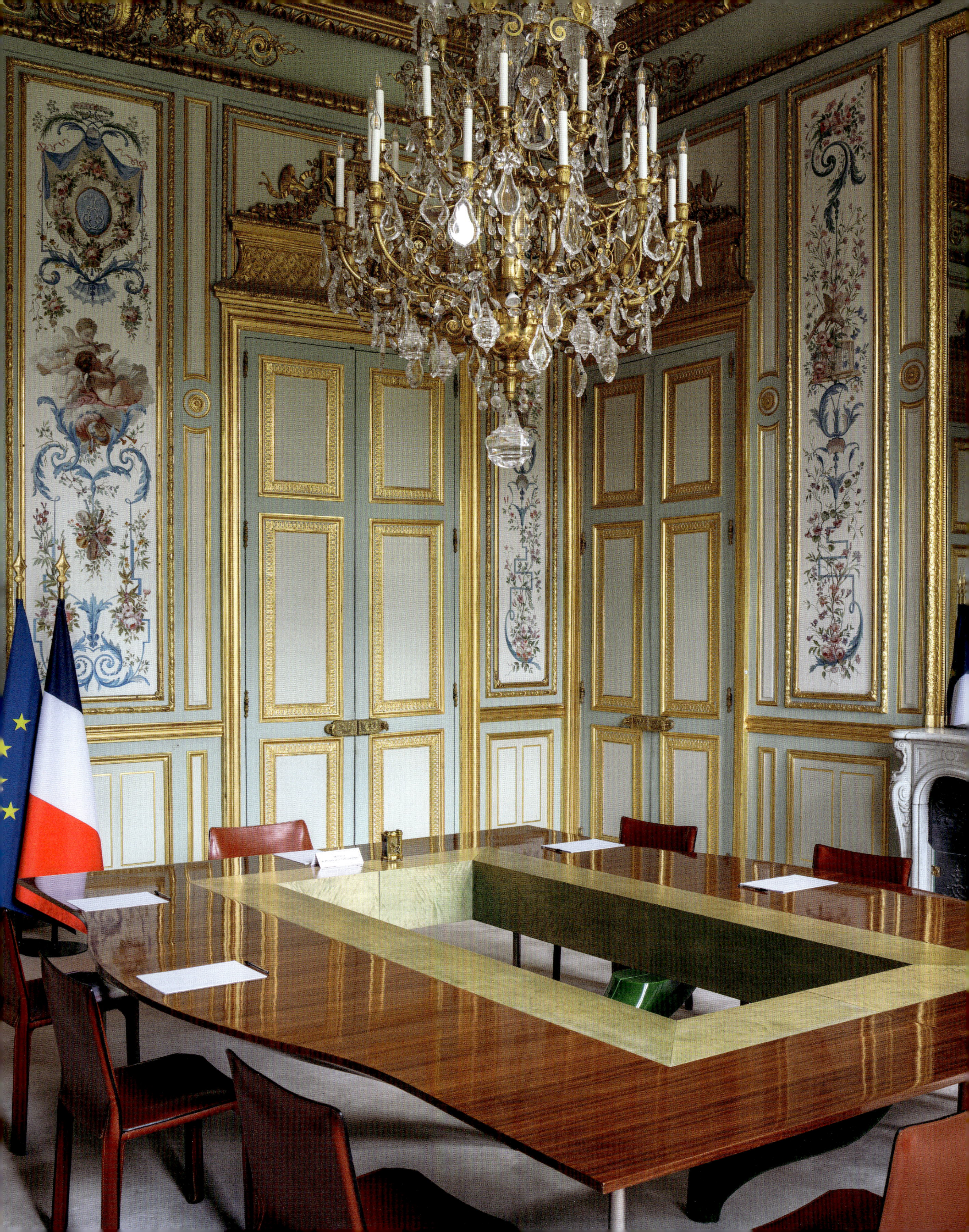

The Green Room

FACING PAGE The Green Room, named after its color during the Second Empire (1852–70), once hosted cabinet meetings. Located next to the president's office, it is used today as a conference room. It is furnished with a conference table by Kristian Gavoille (1996) and Cab chairs by Mario Bellini (1994).

BELOW An Empire-period gilt-bronze clock on the mantelpiece depicts the Fall of Phaeton. The National Furniture Depository boasts a collection of some nine hundred pendulum, wall, and regulator clocks, assembled during the nineteenth century. Masterpieces include this boldly designed, peerlessly chased mantel clock.

"General de Gaulle passed in front of me to enter the Golden Room, and sat behind his desk. He only indicated a chair to me once he was seated. For the previous three years, it had always been the reverse: he would sit only after I was seated; if we went through a door, he made as if to let me go first. Clearly, my status had changed from that of an opposite number, whom he treated with very traditional French courtesy, to that of staff member, whom he treated with blunt hierarchical authority."

Alain Peyrefitte, *C'était de Gaulle*.

The Golden Room

FACING PAGE The Golden Room, with decorative paintwork dating from the Second Empire (1852–70), remained little changed during the Third and Fourth Republics. But ever since Charles de Gaulle became the first president of the Fifth Republic in 1958, it has served as the presidential office where important foreign guests are received. The door handles and chamber locks bearing imperial eagles were changed back in 1898: the eagles were replaced by chased, fire-gilt bronze appliqués of "a head of the Republic with RF monogram and laurel leaves" on the lock box, as well as "an RF breastplate, Gallic rooster, fasces, and palm fronds" for the opposite box. These republican touches were retained when the room was restored to its Second-Empire state.

LA FRANCE

PAGES 176–77, FACING PAGE, AND ABOVE During renovations carried out from 1859 to 1861 by architect Joseph Eugène Lacroix, sculptor Ovide Savreux and painter Jean-Louis Godon were commissioned to decorate this room. It would be misleading to view this room as a typical example of France's "gilded palaces," because here gold is designed to convey the lightness and grace of imperial festivities. The work was probably carried out in a cost-effective way, primarily to create an impression. The overdoors show two putti holding a medallion with the initials of Napoleon III and Eugénie, while the ceiling cornices and coving are decorated with plaster or *carton-pierre* casts of mythological scenes: Diana visiting the sleeping Endymion, Flora crowned by Zephyr, and so on.

The later decision to furnish this room with masterful yet weighty furniture by Boulle and Cressent reflected an anachronistic, paradoxical "idea of France"—one that lasted a long time. Today furnishings include Thierry Lemaire's K desk (2019), Shadow lamps by Caroline Ziegler and Pierre Brichet (2015), Philippe Starck's Passion armchair (2019), and Ico armchairs by Ora-ïto (2018). Against the far wall are two double-column pier tables by Eric Schmitt (2013) on which stand Elancée lamps by Hervé van der Straeten (2003).

BELOW This white marble fireplace was copied in 1860 from the one in the dauphin's bedroom at the Château of Versailles. The gilt-bronze mounts represent Flora and Zephyr, while the medallion in the middle bears Napoleon III's initial. The panels flanking the fireplace are decorated with figures that hardly convey the conventional tone of government—André Malraux, in *Le Miroir des Limbes,* reported that President de Gaulle called them "naked ladies among convolvulus."

FACING PAGE The ironwork on the balcony features a Second-Empire crown. The central position of the Golden Room offers a wonderful view overlooking the garden. French tradition does not include presidents speaking "from the balcony."

RIGHT Two carpets designed by Victor Vasarely, *Light Composition* and *Dark Composition,* play in the light upon the oak parquet floor. They bring a fresh new perspective to the decorative painting by Jean-Louis Godon, which seems to re-emerge for the first time, with its scrolling foliage and dancing women and cherubs set against the gold panels that punctuate the woodwork, including the double-leaf doors, windows overlooking the garden, and the inner shutters.

BELOW In 1896, President Félix Faure completed the installation of electric lighting in all the rooms on the second floor. The current chandelier in the Golden Room was fitted with fifty-six imitation candles when it was wired.

BELOW, RIGHT As usual, the title of the painting by Pierre Soulages is its date, *December 2, 1989*. The black canvas hangs above a pier table by Gilbert Poillerat and two lamps by André Dubreuil. Patrick Jouin's Kami suite of furniture (2005) is complemented by Toni Grilo's Basic set of low coffee tables.

Corner Office

ABOVE Like Valéry Giscard d'Estaing, President Emmanuel Macron decided to install his everyday office in a corner room. FACING PAGE This corner office is furnished with a concrete desk designed by Francesco Passaniti and Mabelle armchairs by Patrick Jouin. On the wall is a Simon Hantaï painting from 1958–59, titled *Painting (Pink Composition)* (Musée National d'Art Moderne, Centre Pompidou, Paris).

The Mirror Room

BELOW Like the other rooms in Princess Eugénie's private apartment, her bathroom (today the Mirror Room) was decorated by Jean-Louis Godon. In his estimate dated 1861, the artist specified that "all the decorative painting [would] imitate the bathroom in the Château of Fontainebleau" (that is to say, the bathroom formerly in the National Furniture Depository, an exquisite example of ornamental painting on glass that had been transferred to Fontainebleau).
FACING PAGE Detail of the scrolling foliage painted onto glass by Godon.

FACING PAGE The eight panels and four overdoors in the Mirror Room were painted on silvered glass in collaboration with Charles Chaplin. For the overdoors, Chaplin depicted mythological figures such as Diana, Leda, and Venus.
ABOVE On the eight panels, Chaplin painted anecdotal figures of different subjects. Seen here is *Fishing*. Other paintings are *The Bath, Flowers, Fruit, The Harvest, The Lovebirds, Hunting*, and *Skating*.

The Ballroom

ABOVE Detail of the ceiling of the Ballroom: a winged putto holding a fan, flanked by the patterned monogram RF.
FACING PAGE The renovation of the Ballroom, resulting in a sophisticated gray and gold décor, was a collaboration between the National Furniture Depository and the Isabelle Stanislas design firm in late 2018–early 2019. One hundred and fifty artisans helped to restore the splendor of this official reception room.

"Why do these refined, sensitive, thoughtful [artists] never attempt to express their vision on larger surfaces, like the old masters, putting their ideas on walls?"

Guillaume Dubufe, discussing artists James Tissot and Luc-Olivier Merson, *Rapport sur l'Exposition Universelle de 1900*.

PAGES 194-95 The ceiling of the Ballroom, painted by Guillaume Dubufe in 1896. In the midst of richly gilded stuccowork, *The Republic Upholding Peace* is flanked by two allegories: Art (shown on the right) and Science.
FACING PAGE Detail of the ceiling in the Ballroom.
PAGES 198-99 Detail of the *The Allegory of Science* by Guillaume Dubufe. As an official painter for the Third Republic, Dubufe was commissioned to decorate many public buildings, such as the theater of the Comédie-Française, the Paris city hall, and the library of the Sorbonne.

RIGHT The Ballroom is lit by eight chandeliers dating from the Second Empire (1852–70), each with fifty-six lights.
At the request of First Lady Brigitte Macron and President Emmanuel Macron, the chandeliers were lowered in order to make the richly decorated ceiling more visible.

"Madame Carnot [the president's wife], wore a silk dress with large black and white stripes, and a fur stole around her shoulders. Her thick, black hair was unadorned. She said, very simply:
'Dear children, thank you very much for having replied to my invitation.... Later I will have the pleasure of giving each of you ... a little booklet, a garment, and a book, plus a gun for the boys and a doll for the girls.'
The children clapped. Then the curtains of the little theater drew back....
Yet people are already saying, 'There were, after all, just 400 of the poor at the party.' But there's nothing stopping the wives of ministers, mayors, and other nay-sayers from following this fine example."

Charles Chincholle, *Le Figaro*, December 26, 1889 (the Ballroom was unveiled the previous May).

FACING PAGE Liberated from heavy red and gold drapes, carved allegorical figures now contribute harmoniously to the light, glittery setting of concerts and grand state dinners.
PAGES 204-5 The ten French windows giving onto the grounds were installed in 1984, during the presidency of François Mitterrand, in order to provide natural lighting.

The "Winter Garden"

LEFT A glass conservatory, or "Winter Garden," was built in 1879 at the initiative of President Jules Grévy, as a transitional space to the garden, which it has ceased to be ever since it became an extension of the Ballroom. It has retained its natural overhead lighting, and is used for official receptions. It was partly renovated in 2018 by the National Furniture Depository and the Isabelle Stanislas design firm.

The Napoleon III Room

BELOW, FACING PAGE, AND PAGES 210–11 The plans for what was originally a ballroom were drawn up by Joseph Eugène Lacroix as early as 1853 but construction wasn't completed until early in the Third Republic (1870). The addition of a "Winter Garden" in 1879 so darkened it that three cupolas were inserted to supply additional light at the request of President Jules Grévy. By turns ballroom, reception room, and dining room, this space has been completely restored, enabling the rich decoration of the high walls and ceiling to be fully appreciated. In the corners of the ceiling, an imperial eagle symbolizing the Second Empire (1852–70) holds the RF monogram ringed by olive and oak branches, symbolizing the French Republic. The chandeliers are identical to those in the Ballroom.

"The presidential palace was naturally the setting for continual visits, parties, and ceremonies. Since nothing is too trivial when it comes to upholding the prestige of the State, I felt it important that in this respect things should be done liberally but with moderation, affably but with dignity."

Charles de Gaulle, *Memoirs of Hope: Renewal, 1958–1962*.

The Pantry

FACING PAGE An Élysée silver steward at work. In the days preceding state dinners, all items of silverware are checked by specialists armed with chamois cloths.

ABOVE Since the eighteenth century, the Sèvres porcelain manufactory has designed and produced ceremonial dinner services of one thousand to one thousand and two hundred pieces for state banquets. On the left is a Sèvres-blue service commissioned from Philippe Favier in 2000 to celebrate the new millennium. On the right is the Diana service designed by Pierre Alechinsky in 2007, based on so-called Diana models created during Georges Pompidou's presidency (1969–74), as decorated by Serge Poliakoff and Yaacov Agam.
LEFT The Élysée Blue service designed by Evariste Richer in 2018.
FACING PAGE Birds service first produced in 1872, with plates imitating ones designed by Duplessis in Vincennes in the eighteenth century from illustrations from Buffon's *Natural History*.

BELOW Setting the table for a presidential lunch.
RIGHT Tall yet portable canteens, or chests of silverware, were designed for presidential voyages. Although that habit is waning, Élysée staff sometimes accompany the head of state elsewhere, for example during sojourns at Brégançon.

BELOW This set of silverware by Puiforcat, a firm founded in 1820, has been in regular use since the 1940s.

ABOVE, LEFT The cupboards in the palace pantry are organized with a rigor worthy of the grandest British stately homes.
ABOVE, RIGHT Every day, the items to be used are placed on a large tray.
FACING PAGE The pantry boasts roughly six thousand pieces of silverware by Christofle and Puiforcat as well as three thousand items of crystal by Baccarat.

N° 1 SERVICE VERMEIL
N° 2 SERVICE VERMEIL
N° 3 SERVICE VERMEIL
42 CUILLERS 36 FOURCHETTES DESSERT
N° 4 SERVICE D'OFFICE
62 FOURCHETTES TABLE
N° 8 SERVICE VERMEIL
N° 9 SERVICE VERM
N° 10 SERVICE VERMEIL
30 CAFÉS 4 CUILLERS SUCRE 6 PINCES SUCRE
N° 12 CASES VIDES
N° 13 CASES VIDES

The Kitchens

FACING PAGE These molds are not collector's items, much less decorative pieces: chefs at the Élysée make a point of continuing to use them from time to time.
BELOW The Élysée's copper pots, some of which bear marks attesting to their long history—here an inscription from the Château of Fontainebleau dates from 1815.

The Gardens

BELOW The grounds of the Élysée are enlivened by a few sculptures, including *Sheep* by François-Xavier Lalanne.
FACING PAGE View of the water feature from the Ballroom.
PAGES 226-27 A grove of greenery to the south of the Ballroom was given a water feature in 1992.

ABOVE View of the patterned boxwood planted in front of the private apartments in the east wing during Valéry Giscard d'Estaing's term of office (1974–81). The small umbrella pine, perhaps one hundred and fifty years old, a gift from Bernadette to Jacques Chirac, was originally found at the far end of the grounds; it was repotted and moved here under Nicolas Sarkozy (2007–12). FACING PAGE Following eighteenth-century custom, a small flower garden was placed near the house, making it easy to compose bouquets. This one has been here since the Count of Évreux first built the residence. The Ballroom can be seen in the background.

FACING PAGE At the request of President François Mitterrand, in 1992 landscape architect Jacques Wirtz restored natural beauty to the five acres of grounds. Their late eighteenth-century state was evoked through curving paths among lawns edged with denser beds of flowers and trees (of which some one hundred varieties were recorded, including two plane trees, perhaps the tallest in Paris, that are over two hundred years old).
BELOW Although the pond was eliminated in 1971, a round reflecting pool with fountain was installed in 1992 on the spot where one had stood in the days of Nicolas Beaujon, providing a focal point for the fine vista.

PAGES 232–33 The terrace, lined with hardy plants that flower at different periods, can be used by the president for working lunches and dinners.
PAGE 234 In 1996, landscape architect Louis Benech tweaked Jacques Wirtz's redesign by reducing the terrace to create more lawn and by planting more vegetation. He also had a small round greenhouse built on the spot where a fashionable grab-the-ring carrousel stood in the late eighteenth century.

PAGE 235 View of the grounds and the south façade of the Élysée as seen from the Gallic Rooster gate.
ABOVE, LEFT Two bronze obelisks (1987) by Ivan Theimer stand at the end of the terrace in front of the Ballroom.
ABOVE, RIGHT *Roots of France* benches by Pablo Reinoso, which have flanked the south terrace since July 2016. The curving metal merges with the beds of greenery where leafy branches of laurel and oak intertwine.

FACING PAGE This monumental bronze stele, some thirteen feet high, was commissioned from artist Ivan Theimer in 1984. The untitled sculpture, crowned by vegetation, rests on four turtles and is adorned with a map of France and other symbols of French history.
PAGES 238-39 A wall to the south—where only the Gallic Rooster gate affords access to Avenue Gabriel—protects the Élysée's green setting from prying eyes. Above it pokes the dome of the Grand Palais in the distance. In a break with tradition, Presidents Chirac and Hollande both chose this setting for their official photograph.

THE PAVILION OF LA LANTERNE

VERSAILLES

At the residence known as La Lanterne, construction vehicles get stuck in the mud, birds warble, and rubber boots are ready for guests—it's the real countryside. You may find a thorn in your side or walk into a hornets' nest, which are also metaphors for political pitfalls. It is rare, however, for France to be actually governed from La Lanterne—Emmanuel Macron withdrew here during his illness in 2020, but that was an exception. The residence is designed to be a weekend retreat for reading and for that other authorized vice, exercise. The people of Versailles, who appreciate this small, tourist-free zone the far end of the Grand Canal, are accustomed to seeing the president leave by a little door equipped with its security camera, in order to jog with a few bodyguards. Although the Grand and Petit Trianons can be found at the end of another branch of the canal on the vast Versailles estate, hasty comparisons should not be made: La Lanterne is not a republican "pleasure house," much less an avatar of Marie-Antoine's hamlet. For example, today La Lanterne has some chickens and goats—received as gifts—but they're where they belong, in farmyard pens, and have no intention of leaving their mark on history.

Reporters always film the guard hut on the road from Saint-Cyr, from whence you can see the gate adorned with the famous stag heads. On the other side, in the grounds, vigilant gardeners have planted "persistent" vegetation to thwart the equally persistent paparazzi. Hybrid green oaks and exotic, bright green quercus from Sierra Madre (the famous Mexican oaks called "maya," which resemble chestnut trees) form a screen that avoids the dark tone usually associated with evergreens.

Little remains of Louis XIV's menagerie—a traditional royal distraction (Charles V had one at Vincennes)—designed in the 1660s and splendidly equipped at the very end of the seventeenth century. There survive just two pavilions and a few vestiges among the tall grasses, such as the surprising "elephant circle." Nearby buildings include a few lodgings that still belong to the Versailles complex and La Lanterne itself, a "pavilion" originally occupied by the dukes of Noailles, who were hereditary governors of the Château of Versailles. In 1787, Prince Philippe de Noailles, Duke of Poix and Duke of Mouchy, made Marshal of France in 1775, and son of the woman whom Marie-Antoinette anxiously nicknamed "Madame Etiquette," had this handsome house built. Full of windows like a "lantern," it visually echoed the architectural lantern on the cupola of the menagerie. The architect's name remains unknown. The independent property, covering somewhat less than ten acres, is enclosed by high walls.

There was nothing lavish about this elegant hunting lodge, which was sold during the Revolution but bought by the nation once again in 1818, during the Restoration, when Louis XVIII was considering revamping Versailles. The government initially allocated it to the commander of the nearby military academy of Saint-Cyr, then to François-Xavier-Félix Jourdain, the inspector of forest and royal hunts, and himself a great deer hunter.

The lodge was later rented to the famous James Gordon Bennett, Jr., the brilliant son of the founder of the *New York Herald*. Bennett established the Gordon Bennett balloon-race cup and himself founded the *Paris Herald* (later the *New York Herald Tribune* as sold by Jean Seberg on the Champs-Élysée in Jean-Luc Godard's film *Breathless*). General de Gaulle, who had no desire to use it when he was head of the provisional French government during the Liberation, allocated La Lanterne to Prime Minister Michel Debré in 1959. That decision disappointed Jacques Chaban-Delmas, president of the National Assembly, who had hoped to move in after André Le Troquer, the previous president of the Assembly. But Le Troquer had rented the property on a personal basis, following David K. E. Bruce, the U.S. ambassador (and the "last American aristocrat" according to his biographer), who lived in La Lanterne from 1949 to 1957.

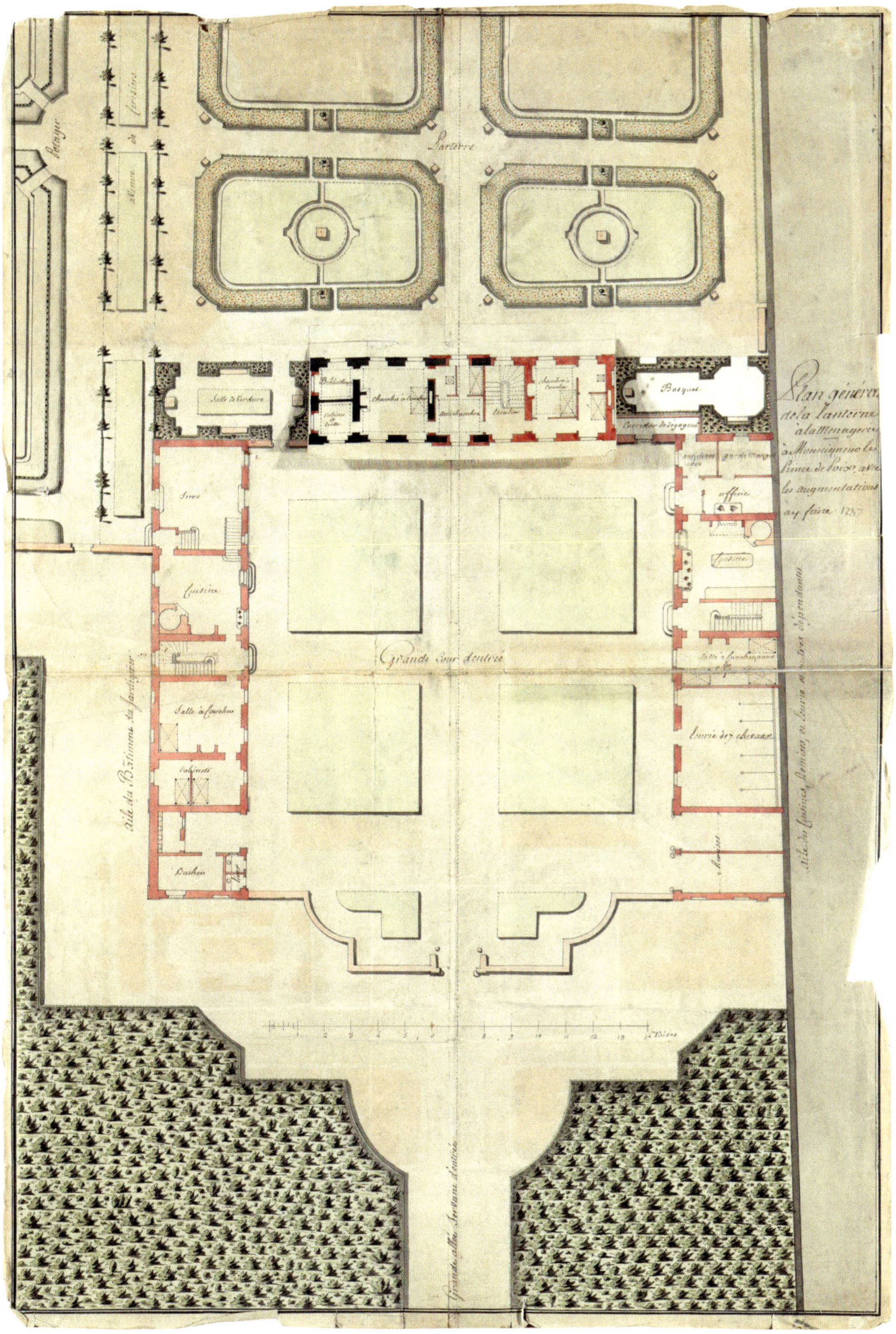

PAGE 240 This pediment on the façade of La Lanterne features ornamental details typical of the eighteenth century. Here quiver and gun indicate that the building was a hunting lodge.
PAGE 241 A lane lined with poplar trees leads to a stag-headed gate. The nine-acre estate is ringed by a wall.
RIGHT An overall plan, from 1787, of the pavilion of La Lanterne, near the menagerie at Versailles, to house the superintendant of the Versailles estate, Prince Philippe de Noailles, Duke of Poix. Noailles, Captain of the Royal Hunt, had La Lanterne built two years before the French Revolution began. In 1789 he sat as a nobleman at the Estates General.

A major restoration campaign was then carried out, thanks to the talents of Marc Saltet, an architect with the Versailles estate. That was when the side buildings, which had been used as stables, kitchens, and storehouses, were comfortably fitted out (an old dairy, with marble walls and table, still survives in the service wing). Louis-XVI furnishings mingled with Empire decoration, and Nattier-blue velvet harmonized with shantung wall linings. Debré installed his office in a large room of the left wing, which today serves as a drawing room to house President Macron's piano and piles of music scores. Debré then ceded use of La Lanterne to André Malraux, the French minister of culture, from 1961 to 1969, a gesture that not only honored the great writer whom de Gaulle liked to have at his side, but also offered protection to a man whose apartment in Boulogne was blown up in 1962 by traitorous officers conspiring against the government's Algerian policy. Malraux was not happy, however, in this setting, which seemed more suited to an eighteenth-century play by Marivaux.

Yet Malraux made La Lanterne his sole residence for seven years, surrounded by his books, papers, and cats Olympe and Octave (as photographed by Gisèle Freund). His wife, Madeleine, a spirited pianist, vainly tried to turn the home into a music pavilion. They brought in fireside armchairs known as *confortables* and hung faille-weave curtains in red or subtle gray tastefully trimmed with green. The National Furniture Depository supplied them with a "Paris suite" of furniture designed by Raoul Dufy—chairs, armchairs, sofas, and screen—which had been sitting in store since 1933. Other furnishings were designed by André Groult, while tapestries depicted the sights of Paris (the Concorde obelisk flanked by the Marly horses, Notre-Dame Cathedral, and the Eiffel Tower). Groult's art deco style arrived rather late, but it sought to give La

Lanterne an air of fun around the Pleyel double-keyboard grand piano that dated from the Internationl Exposition of 1937 and for which Madeleine had paid just "a fistful of cherries." In vain were these attempts to brighten a home that always seems somewhat sad to visitors.

After Madeleine and André Malraux separated, Louise de Vilmorin moved in with André and made fun of the fairy-tale house to her niece Sophie. "What's amazing is that La Lanterne belongs to the government, so you can chose furniture from the National Furniture Depository. One week you feel like living in the Empire style, delightful men in overalls arrive with trucks and change everything. A week later, you'd like medieval or Restoration furniture, and it's done." She was obviously exaggerating. The Empire furniture dated from the Debré era, and although it had indeed been replaced, La Lanterne could hardly rival the flawless taste of the blue drawing room in Vilmorin's own family home in Verrières-le-Buisson.

Today the Louise de Vilmorin style still seems to linger in a bedroom under the eaves, with its white-washed roof timbers, blue furniture, and embroidered floral bedhead. What "Marilyn Malraux"—Vilmorin's own nickname for herself—hadn't foreseen was that Jacques Chaban-Delmas, having become prime minister in 1969, would furnish it in a modern style. Historian Fabien Oppermann interpreted Chaban-Delmas's initiative (based on the testimony of Alain Malraux, who saw both versions) as a desire to rival President Pompidou's modernization of the Élysée through the use of "tulip chairs, furniture in metal and plastic, and Plexiglas." (Pompidou himself, when serving as prime minister, had had no desire to use La Lanterne because he owned a country home in

FACING PAGE André Malraux with one of his cats on the grounds of La Lanterne, where he lived for seven years. This photo of the famous author and minister of culture was taken by Gisèle Freund, who had fled Germany in 1933; in 1981 she would take the official photo of President François Mitterrand in the Library of the Élysée Palace.
ABOVE The Paris suite of furniture by Raoul Dufy includes armchairs, chairs, a sofa, and this screen. It had all been in store since 1933, but Madeleine Malraux, a talented pianist, hoped this furniture would create the atmosphere of a music room at La Lanterne.

Orvilliers and also liked his family farm in Cajarc.) A subsequent period of renovation work was carried out by Prime Minister Michel Rocard (1988–91), who added a tennis court and swimming pool (which now requires renovation itself, having become a part of the national heritage associated with the site).

Nicolas Sarkozy moved in as soon as was he elected president in 2007, politely banishing his prime minister to the uncomfortable, uninhabitable Château of Rambouillet (a former hunting retreat where the first G6 summit was held in 1975) and to another nationally owned property in Souzy-la-Briche, where President Mitterrand had housed his mistress, Anne Pingeot, and their secret daughter. Pingeot wittily opined that the country house was "nineteenth-century ugly, but that doesn't matter." These days no one uses it, not even prime ministers.

La Lanterne, meanwhile, was built so quickly that it needs regular work. Below it runs a stream that flows from one of the springs feeding the Grand Canal at Versailles, so the basement is damp, the walls were long cracked, and a ceiling even collapsed on Malraux's manuscripts in 1967. Things are better today, however.

The grounds need no ornament. A cast-iron copy of the statue of Diana at Versailles stands alone in a grove (and would be at home in any municipal park). The only interesting artwork is a fine marble statue of Empress Joséphine, titled *Meditation*, a copy of an original by François Joseph Bosio. It stands behind the "Rocard swimming pool," a white figure inspired by ancient depictions of modest Venus, with a yew hedge for a backdrop.

The first glimpse is "very French," which can be explained by the fact that the grounds were redesigned by a Café-Society American in the twentieth century. A parcel of landscape garden seems to have been pushed to one side, where people pick mushrooms near a temporary soccer goal that looks like it's there to stay. In the middle, four square patches of lawn unfold like a picnic cloth. The grass used to be cut with a sickle, old-style. It's a true French lawn, that is to say with weeds, daisies, and buttercups—the opposite of an English lawn.

Since the Malraux period, the grounds have taken on a certain patina. On a sunny June day, or on an evening when new lighting is being tested on the façade, the property seems to embody a carefree lifestyle. The only serious intrusion is made by ladybugs: these good-luck symbols, which come from the lab of a nearby agricultural institute, do constant battle against aphids. Meanwhile, round balls of box, regularly invaded by moss and ivy, have been cleared and pruned to restore their fine, appealing air.

La Lanterne is no Camp David, the Shangri-La retreat appreciated by almost all American presidents since Eisenhower. No cabinet meeting is ever held here, nor are international agreements signed here. So if the French president receives a privileged visitor or foreign head of state at La Lanterne, it's a little like President de Gaulle hosting German chancellor Konrad Adenauer at his own home of La Boisserie. The private dwelling then becomes the most publicized one—the absence of protocol becomes the highest protocol. It has been the fate of every alternative venue to Versailles, starting with Marly under Louis XIV, to become a super Versailles from time to time, when a lack of pomp indicates the height of privilege. It is a political trump card to be played sparingly, at just the right moment.

The same is not quite true of the other supposedly private presidential residence in France, the Fort of Brégançon.

FACING PAGE One of the statues on the grounds is a recent copy of a nymph from the famous Baths of Apollo Grove at Versailles.

ABOVE The stag heads on the near gate were sculpted by Claude Poirier in 1703 for the menagerie at Versailles, then restored in 1785–86. It is unclear whether they were placed here when La Lanterne was built in 1787 or when James Gordon Bennett, Jr., revamped the premises in 1891.
FACING PAGE The central façade of La Lanterne offers a glimpse, in the distance, of a recent copy of one of the nymphs from the famous Baths of Apollo Grove at Versailles.
PAGES 250–51 The simplicity of this building with a courtyard in front and a garden in back embodies the essence of an elegant, French-style home, which greatly appealed to the American tenants who first began to restore the premises.

FACING PAGE The road from Versailles to Saint-Cyr passes just in front of the little white gate in the distance. **ABOVE, LEFT** This statue, titled *Meditation,* is a copy by Jean Lagrange of one by François Joseph Bosio, allegedly based on Empress Joséphine. It recalls the conventional pose of ancient depictions of a modest Venus, and seems well placed by the pool built when Prime Minister Michel Rocard occupied the premises. **ABOVE, RIGHT** This fair nymph is a resin and marble powder cast of a sculpture by Thomas Regnaudin for the Grotto of Thetis at Versailles. The original sculpted group of Apollo attended by nymphs, completed by Regnaudin and François Girardon in 1675, is one of the finest examples of seventeenth-century sculpture. In 1781 Hubert Robert designed a rocky grove to harbor these statues. Copies were recently made of two of the nymphs to enhance the views at La Lanterne.

"Our monuments are France's greatest dream.... That is why we must save them: not for the curiosity or admiration of tourists—which is not unimportant—but for the emotion stirred in children we take by the hand..... We shall ensure that all French children will some day realize that these stones, still very much alive, will belong to them providing they continue to love them! Some day we shall bury, alongside the statue of either Mansart or Louis XIV, one of the unknown masons who built Versailles, and—thanks to the law I am asking you to pass today—we shall carve on his tombstone: 'To Versailles, built for the king, won by the people, saved by the nation.'"

André Malraux, Minister of Culture, July 31, 1962, from a speech to the National Assembly.

FACING PAGE The gardeners who tend these box plants are careful to give them somewhat dissimilar shapes and to leave the lawn looking fairly natural, as distinct from the rigor of British lawns.
PAGES 256-57 The architect of this pavilion, which had no official function at the time, remains unknown. After the Revolution, it became national property and was sold off.

ABOVE This luminous entrance hall provides access to the main reception room, dining room, and office on the ground floor.
RIGHT The entrance hall features two paintings by Claude Viallat that echo the traditional black-and-white tiled floor. To the right a staircase leads upstairs, while the far end opens onto the dining room (near the kitchen wing) and a small living room.

RIGHT A marble sculpture by Michèle Forgeois, *Nymph* (1981), and a painting by Hugo Schüwer-Boss, *Extra-ball* (2008), grace the dining room.

ABOVE Graceful bisque figurines of Psyche and the Three Graces find their place on the mantelpiece of this resolutely modern living room.
RIGHT On the piano in the living room are scores by Schubert and Ravel. The painting by Alessandro Mendini, done in 1999, is on loan from the CNAP, the national visual arts center, as are most of the modern works hanging on the walls.

W.HOFFMANN

LIFE
NAPOLI

"Lucien was surprised to find that the windows of his office looked out over a lovely garden, and it struck him as a curious contrast to the barrenness of his recent sensations. He gazed tenderly down upon the trees."

Stendhal, *Lucien Leuwen: The Telegraph*.

FACING PAGE The president's office is also his library, but there are books in every room of La Lanterne these days. The Strates desk was designed by Mathieu Lehanneur (2012), while the Cyborg PLY chairs are by Marcel Wanders (2016).

BELOW La Lanterne is a house of transparency, always open to new viewpoints on the architecture and the constant interplay of geometric lines.
FACING PAGE The row of rooms leading from one to another is a charming feature of La Lanterne, designed for ordinary family life, including recently made "period" furniture that makes no attempt to fool anyone.
PAGES 268-69 A 1977 painting by Lorris Junec lights up this drawing room. The books on the coffee table include the catalogue of a Delacroix exhibition at the Louvre.

Louis Juriec 1977

BELOW The white-washed roof timbers of this bedroom under the eaves, with its blue furniture and flower-embroidered bedhead, seem to incarnate the spirit of novelist Louise de Vilmorin, who lived at La Lanterne with André Malraux in the 1960s.
FACING PAGE View of the stairway leading to the bedrooms.

ABOVE La Lanterne is located on the edge of the royal estate of Versailles, at the end of one of the branches of the Grand Canal, opposite the Trianons. The denizens of Versailles who stroll and jog along these lanes are accustomed to encountering the president and his bodyguards.
FACING PAGE One of the two small, surviving buildings of the former menagerie at Versailles, on the edge of the grounds of La Lanterne.

THE FORT OF BRÉGANÇON

BORMES-LES-MIMOSAS

Why did the French government lumber itself with a "fort," a beguiling seaside residence where you can't even go swimming? This democratic rock makes no claim to rival the princely rock of Monaco, yet it triggers all kinds of fantasies about some inaccessible, independent realm. (In fact, it frequently hosts guided tours when the president isn't in residence.)

The peninsula has its own microclimate. The ground is very dry, yet everything is humid, making a true botanical garden of this rocky clump in the sea. Rare species live in harmony with olive and laurel trees, umbrella pines, Aleppo pines, and recently introduced lemon trees (in pots). The fort is not a legacy of the French monarchy, although it boasts is own worthy heritage: Charles IX passed through in 1564 with his mother, Queen Catherine de' Medici; Napoleon Bonaparte made a coastal inspection tour here after his first brilliant military victory, the siege of Toulon; and later, during the Empire, Napoleon turned it into a small garrison of veterans.

Right from the ninth century there existed a medieval military post at Brégançon, although located on the mainland, where a vineyard exists today (as can be seen when taking Avenue Tézenas along the coast). It was only in the fifteenth century that defensive works were built on the islet, which belonged to the marquisate of Iles d'Or, a handsome title that King Francis I bestowed on his Master of Ships. In the late sixteenth century, Brégançon belonged to the king, who nevertheless sold it to Boniface de la Mole (a name appropriated by Stendhal for his novel *The Red and the Black*). It later came into the Honoré de Gasqui family, who modernized the towers.

In 1919 the French army abandoned the site and the government rented out the fort, which required renovation. Robert Bellanger, a left-of-center politician from Ille-et-Vilaine in the north, who had served as undersecretary of the navy under Prime Minister Camille Chautemps in 1930, rented what may have looked

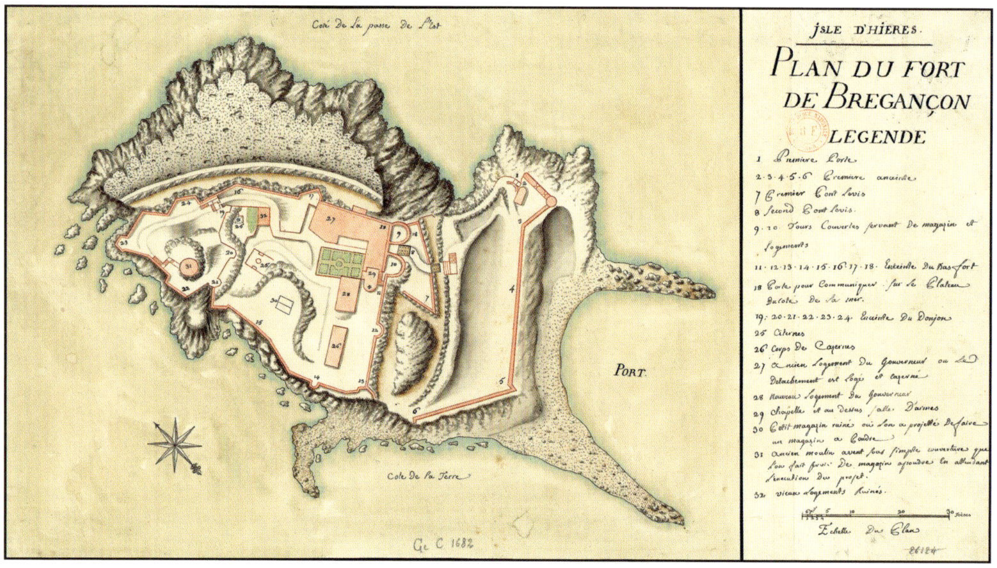

PAGE 274 The view of the Mediterranean Sea from the balcony of the president's bedroom.
PAGE 275 View of Brégançon with its fortified entrance.
LEFT *Plan of the Fort of Brégançon*, eighteenth century (Bibliothèque Nationale de France, Paris).
FACING PAGE Brégançon was a look-out post whose defensive towers have been made quite pleasant: this little balcony was added in the twentieth century to turn a military fort into a seaside residence.

to him like a mini-version of Saint-Malo, minus the rain. He and his family happily lived there until 1963, when he was suddenly informed that his lease would not be renewed. A wealthy man (as co-founder of Bellanger Automobiles, a maker of splendid, gas-guzzling cars until it was taken over by Peugeot), Bellanger loved to host his friends in the fort that he had restored with great taste. He notably had running water put in. (The island, which has no spring, could not really withstand a siege and had quickly capitulated in 1524 when the Duke of Bourbon attacked it on behalf of Holy Roman Emperor Charles V.) Bellanger also had electricity installed, so that modern life could begin. He furthermore built the causeway, the road, and the picturesque outer wall that evokes, at sunset, the Saharan location of Pierre Benoit's fantasy novel *Atlantida*. It was thus Bellanger who turned an uncomfortable fortress, reinforced in the late nineteenth century, into a gem perched upon a picture-perfect Mediterranean setting. Perhaps General de Gaulle appreciated Bellanger's 1930s taste; or maybe he enjoyed the account of the capture of the Fort of Brégançon by Captain de Leusse at the end of World War II; or the lack of beach may have appealed. (Can you imagine de Gaulle on a beach?) Whatever the case, nowhere did the general explain his reasons for making the Fort of Brégançon a presidential residence.

He spent just one night there, before celebrating the twentieth anniversary, on August 15, 1964, of the Allied landing in Provence. That was the basis of his decision to turn Brégançon into a residence for French heads of state. Perhaps he wanted to assert France's attachment, as a Mediterranean power, to this outpost. Yet having made the decision, de Gaulle himself never returned.

Renovation of the fort was completed by 1968. A job that might have called for the sober genius of Pierre Barbe—who reinvented a modern Provençal style for Annette Schlumberger's estate at Les Treilles—went to a skillful naval architect, Pierre-Jean Guth, who enlarged, streamlined, and modernized the site, building a guest wing while retaining its mildly monastic air. He did not go so far as to surf the *Captain Blood/Iron Mask* wave, which was all the rage among castles following the 1960s movies in which Jean Marais dashed and leaped through white-washed archways as the bad guys crumpled to the tiled floor. Listed as a national monument in 1968, Brégançon was furnished by the National Furniture Depository the better to host President Pompidou and his wife for five years. The fort thus unobtrusively began to play a new role. The guard still fires a small canon and raises the colors every morning, but there where de Gaulle envisaged another garrison—another rock of the French Republic—the new presidential couple saw a perfect vacation home where the family could spend time with friends, playing petanque in sandals, going to Mass at the church of Saint-Trophyme in Bormes-les-Mimosas, and having relaxed lunches with the likes of Pierre Soulages and Françoise Sagan. Just opposite was the island of Porquerolles, which in 1891–92, along with the Iles d'Or, inspired Henri-Edmond Cross to paint one of his finest works. This vibrant canvas, now in the Musée d'Orsay, was a harbinger of abstraction and once belonged to critic Félix Fénéon before it was acquired by the nation in 1947. Although the fort has no boat and no real beach (despite regular attempts since 1972 to build a sea wall constantly undermined by currents), it has a magical view and pleasant sea breezes.

President Giscard d'Estaing sent almost all the Paulin-designed furniture back to Paris, turning Brégançon into a Provençal family home where solid armchairs and commodes, again supplied by the National Furniture Depository, set the tone. A tiny beach reached by a very steep stairway along the rock face enabled France's first sporty president to go swimming. Super-8 movies were made of the children, later providing proof that Jacques Chirac hadn't been as poorly received there as he had claimed.

The fort has only two neighbors. Sarrazin Tower houses the family of the grand dukes of Luxembourg, and enjoys extraterritorial status that extends as far as the road, making the property the grand duchy's only coastline. Queen Jean is the home of the legendary commander Paul-Louis Weiller, a war hero, art patron, member of the Académie des Beaux-Arts, and collector of fine houses and good friends—in 1994 his grand-daughter Sibilla married Prince William of Luxembourg. The French president never fails to entertain these princely neighbors.

Faithful to Pompidou's memory, President Chirac also stayed at Brégançon, which his wife liked. The Chiracs reinforced the classic French taste that some interior decorators laughingly call "Provençal Gustavian." President Nicolas Sarkozy, however, preferred nearby Cap Nègre, while President François Hollande shunned the fort entirely, temporarily authorizing the Historic Monuments Center to open it to the public—an option that had already worked at Rambouillet.

Comparing the current state of the Fort of Brégançon to old photographs, it seems like a whole new window has been opened. An above-ground pool among the greenery finally makes swimming possible—which doesn't exclude undersea diving with mask and snorkel (after having swum across Luxembourg's territorial waters). The flowery curtains are gone, as are the floral and olive-branched carpets. Paulin's Élysée lamp seems at home beneath the pure vaulted ceilings, while his red, white, and blue Amphis sofa—designed for the French pavilion at the Osaka International Exposition in 1970—is a kind of allusion to Pompidou; it seems as though it has been there forever, when in fact it arrived when the fort was managed by the National Monuments Center. The bedsteads are gone, but Paulin's large, module shelving stretches along one wall, while the curves of his big table and chairs harmonize with the interior volumes. In the president's office—connected to the bedroom via a rather theatrical staircase with half-landing—a tapestry by Geneviève Asse seems to echo the large canvas that similarly imparts a horizon to the cabinet meeting room in the Élysée.

The office and bedroom overlook the sea in a spare setting that matches the spirit of the place. The bedrooms of the aide-de-camp, physician, and chief of staff remain spartan with their iron beds and shower stalls. The former chapel, which has long served as the TV room (and probably will until "the tube" finally vanishes), now hosts the blue furniture Mitterrand used in his Élysée office. There thus reigns over the fort a subtle presidential idiom composed of references to features henceforth considered historical.

The most striking thing is the variety of viewpoints. A table placed on the belvedere can be used for work or meals, while another table, next to the cannon beneath the French flag, offers a different view along the coastline. Brégançon, now completely connected, thus enables the head of state to work differently, from different angles.

FACING PAGE, TOP President Georges Pompidou and his wife, Claude, enjoyed vacationing here, where they would invite friends, artists, and sometimes even reporters.

FACING PAGE, BOTTOM President and Madame Giscard d'Estaing willingly showed off their sportiness at Brégançon.

PAGES 280-81 The Republican Guard on duty at the Fort of Brégançon during a visit by German chancellor Angela Merkle on August 20, 2020. The Guard's elite regiments perform several important roles, including protection of the president as well as attendance at ceremonial events. On occasion, a cavalry squadron–one of the French army's last and most glorious mounted units–will even dismount.

G42

PAGES 282–83 The Fort of Brégançon perches high above the sea on a rocky promontory connected to the mainland by a causeway.
ABOVE The lane leading to the fortified entrance. In 1564 the fort hosted King Charles IX and his mother, Queen Catherine de' Medici.
FACING PAGE The lane leading up to the entrance was made considerably more attractive when the fort was rented and lavishly decorated by Robert Bellanger, a sun-loving politician from the north of France.

"A secret was attaching me to the fortress, like a child to some hiding place. . . ."

Julien Gracq, *The Opposing Shore*.

FACING PAGE According to tour guides, this fortified entrance is what most impresses the small groups taken there by the local tourist office in Bormes-les-Mimosas. **PAGES 288–89** The courtyard and main living quarters were soberly redesigned by a fine naval architect, Pierre-Jean Guth. The courtyard is paved with black and ocher pebbles from the Durance river, in geometric patterns inspired by the Alcázar in Seville.

PAGE 290 The French windows, installed during the Mitterrand presidency (1981–95), created a vestibule where a covered porch once met the main courtyard. The guest house on the right was added when the fort became a presidential residence.

PAGE 291 The incline leading to the promontory gives little sign that this strategic site was the setting for a military exploit by Captain François de Leusse during World War II. The recent addition of potted lemon trees adds another fragrance to this Mediterranean garden.

ABOVE, LEFT The exotic-looking entrance gate adds to Brégançon's mystery.

ABOVE, RIGHT These stairs lead to a small terrace overlooking the sea, where a table can be set for a lunch overheard by no one but the birds.

FACING PAGE The apparently wind-worn crenellations were added in the twentieth century, creating the poetic air of some long-abandoned island.

PAGE 294–95 The beach, highly prized by French paparazzi.
FACING PAGE The blue furniture in the living room (once a chapel) was originally designed by Pierre Paulin for the Élysée office of President Mitterand during his second term (1988–95).
ABOVE View looking toward Porquerolles and the Iles d'Or.

BELOW Furniture by Pierre Paulin, which first appeared here during Pompidou's term (1969–74), has returned once again. A "back-to-back" sofa of steel upholstered in beige jersey fabric (1968) accompanies chairs and lamps designed for the Élysée Palace.
FACING PAGE This famous lamp by Paulin, known as his Élysée design, stands next to an untitled oil painting by Éric Dalbis (2003).
PAGES 300–301 This red, white, and blue Amphis sofa (designed by Pierre Paulin for the Osaka International Exposition in 1970) was not originally intended for the fort, but was placed in the large entrance hall when the premises were opened to guided tours. It now sets the overall tone. On the wall hangs an oil painting by Pierre Fichet, *Homage to Jean Mermoz* (1969).

"The house and location are superb. You have a front-row view of the sea and benefit from the breeze."

President Georges Pompidou, *Lettres, Notes et Portraits, 1928–1974*.

FACING PAGE The living room is furnished with a sofa and armchairs designed by Andrée Putman, walnut-topped Pebble coffee tables (Cinna, 2017), and lamps and side table by Pierre Paulin. Over the mantelpiece is a painting by André Maurice, *Space Variations No. 6* (1982). From the ceiling hangs a Coco chandelier designed by Coralie Beauchamp for the National Furniture Depository in 2019.

RIGHT In the dining room, three works (all 2011) by Samuel Richardot hang above a rococo, Louis-XV-period pier table.

BELOW The bathroom in the president's apartment has retained its 1970s decoration.
FACING PAGE The upstairs hallway with its red earthenware tiles leads to the spartan bedrooms allocated to guests.

PAGES 308-9 Upstairs, the presidential office has been relieved of its curtains and old furniture. It now hosts a suite of cherrywood furniture—desk, chairs, and round table—designed by Richard Peduzzi in 2004. The carpet, commissioned from Pierre Paulin by President Mitterrand, sparks a dialogue with a small tapestry by Geneviève Asse (not visible here). The small, framed poster on the far wall—published by an association that promotes local government—shows the successive presidents of France.
FACING PAGE AND BELOW This spot is probably at its most enchanting at night: the sound of the sea, the scent of pines, and the play of light and shadow create a poetic Mediterranean setting.

THREE RESIDENCES, THREE VISIONS

Should the French presidency abandon the Élysée Palace? President de Gaulle apparently considered three other residences (the École Militaire, Les Invalides, and the Château of Vincennes), but never actually moved, perhaps because all three were perfect targets for public demonstrations: the large squares and lawns in front of those historic buildings would have provided terrific photo opportunities for the uprisings of May '68! But maybe it was also because all three have highly visible chapels, making any transformation into a secular residence difficult. Or maybe the ghosts of Louis XIV (École Militaire), Napoleon (Les Invalides), and Charles V (Vincennes) loomed heavier than that of Madame de Pompadour.

The Élysée, La Lanterne, and the Fort of Brégançon share the advantage of never having been royal. Brégançon is neither a two-towered Windsor Castle nor a Balmoral by the Mediterranean. La Lanterne was just a hunting lodge of unpredictable destiny. And while the Élysée was an imperial palace, it was never really part of the "monarchic tradition" of which French presidents remain so wary. Yet neither do these residences have the democratic simplicity of 10 Downing Street or Bessastaðir (Iceland's charming presidential home, formerly a schoolhouse). Furthermore, they are the antithesis of the white, empty rooms of the German Chancellery in Berlin, which in many ways is a model—if unfairly disparaged—of a modern governmental residence. Berlin seems like a dream to French advisers fed up with tiny offices and the absence of real conference rooms. However, one of the advantages of the Élysée, despite the overused cliché of "gilded prison," is that a discreet escape is always possible.

When furnishing the Élysée, several options exist. One involves reconstituting an idealized original state (without, obviously, eliminating the most striking later additions—no one would think of removing the portraits encased in the wood paneling of the Portrait Room or of demolishing the Ballroom). That was the spirit adopted by Giscard d'Estaing, who underscored the successive strata of uninterrupted occupation, almost like an archeologist. Another possibility involves making a real mark, as the Auriols and Pompidous did, all the while ensuring, with perhaps sincere modesty, that any changes could be undone. Finally, President Sarkozy and now President Macron have tended to favor its immaterial, as well as material, heritage.

Perhaps, prior to becoming president, some politicians dreamed of what they would do if they ever entered the Élysée, when they were still young palace advisers (as were Giscard d'Estaing, Hollande, and Macron), or when they were received there as head of the opposition party (as were Mitterrand and Chirac). We might even wonder what famous political leaders who never lived there would have made of the Élysée. Would Georges Clémenceau (prime minister, 1906–09 and 1917–20) have bedecked it with Asian art and paintings by Monet? Would Marie-Claire, wife of Prime Minister Pierre Mendès-France (1954–55), have sought to reproduce the spirit of the elegant Provençal interiors of her family château at Montfrin? Might Edmonde Charles-Roux, a journalist and author as well as the wife of influential Minister of the Interior Gaston Defferre (1981–86), have called in the designers promoted by *Vogue Paris,* of which she was editor-in-chief? Anne Pingeot, mistress of François Mitterrand (1981–95) and a specialist in nineteenth-century sculpture, might have turned the palace grounds into an historic sculpture garden.

With every new election, every new president is confronted with the same paradox of trying to leave a mark while knowing that he is merely "the occupant of the Élysée" (as the press likes to refer to the president), knowing that maybe nothing will survive refurbishments and embellishments that inevitably spark cries of both admiration (among courtiers) and criticism (because too expensive, too modern—or not modern enough). At a time when various periods are superimposed and juxtaposed, can the Élysée possibly serve as the showcase for some brand-new style? In his books, *Les Styles* and *Les Collectionneurs*, the merciless critic Philippe Jullian invented a character named Madame Haugoult-Dujour who would proudly assert, "It's my own little patch of extravagance." All first ladies—until the day that role is filled by a first gentleman unable to do any better than they—privately dread resembling Mrs. Currant-Crayze.

Stylistically, there are two inherent pitfalls: the barracks style and the prefecture style. A third risk is the foolish idea of trying to reconcile the two, resulting in the embassy style. The barracks style—or to be more accurate, the "commander's residence style"—has left its mark on the building insofar as many officers, gendarmes, and firemen are regularly on duty there. For Charles and Yvonne de Gaulle, moving into the Élysée was like yet another posting to a long list of barracks. Neither the first couple nor the military felt out of place—the dozens of offices in the side wings were full of little imitation Louis-XVI tables, indoor plants, and worn staircase carpets typical of a colonel's lodgings on some air-force base. This neutral style was also imposed by the minister of defense on the naval offices on Place de la Concorde, then housed in the former premises of the National Furniture Depository until the building was listed as a national monument and carefully restored with a view to opening it to the public.

The prefecture style is perhaps worse, because in every region of France it triggers a somewhat vague, mythical image of the French presidency: shouldn't every "prefect's mansion" contain an apartment always ready to receive the nation's president? The Louis-XVI style of prefecture building is a Louis-XVI mansion that never had the luck to be distilled by the likes of Christian Dior (who notoriously took an oval-back chair upholstered in pearl gray—the height of elegance in his mother's day—and made it his trademark). The prefecture style has useless furniture (sofas where no one ever lounges and chairs suited for a waiting room), accompanied by incomprehensible tapestries and pendant chandeliers. It oozes an outmoded air that kills, in advance, all conversation—the very art that France brought into this world.

The embassy style, meanwhile, has produced some successes in Belgrade and South Africa, yet has also yielded French-inspired interiors in Bucharest and Montevideo featuring utterly useless marble-topped gilt-wood side tables, little equestrian statues of Louis XIV in bronze, and the predictable juxtaposition of an eighteenth-century commode below an abstract painting by the likes of Olivier Debré. In the past ten years, however, the embassy style has been improving.

In the twenty-first century, the three presidential homes have acquired a certain unity. There is a stronger complementarity, beyond the merely picturesque, between the main dwelling and the two annexes. The functions and signs of government have evolved—there is no longer a need for a hunting lodge (*exit* Rambouillet), although the idea of a nature-loving president in the groves near Versailles or on the shores of the Mediterranean also corresponds to a political agenda. Current restorations (long overdue), along with recent refurnishings, assert the fairly new idea that these premises shall not remain frozen in time. These walls have hosted so many "temporary guests"—in a nod to André Malraux's *Hôtes de Passage*, which opens with his conversations with Léopold Sédar Senghor—that they are always eager for new tales. They remain open to the forging of as-yet unnamed styles, of unforeseen traditions, and of histories yet to be written.

PAGES 314–15 Door handles with emblems of the French Republic in the Aides-de-Camp Room.

R
F

SELECTED BIBLIOGRAPHY

Among a wide range of references—including primary sources, first-hand accounts, and political anecdotes, not to mention scholarly studies of architecture and the decorative arts—the following were particularly useful during the writing of this book:

BERSANI, Marie-Hélène, and Thierry SARMANT with the assistance of the Mobilier National. *Les Métiers d'art du Mobilier national.* Paris: Gallimard/Mobilier national, 2020.

BLONDEL, Jacques François. *Architecture françoise, ou Recueil des plans, élévations, coupes et profils des églises, maisons royales, palais, hôtels et édifices les plus considérables de Paris.* Vol. III. Paris: Chez Charles-Antoine Jombert, 1752–1756.

CORDEY, Jean, ed. *Inventaire des biens de Madame de Pompadour, rédigé après son décès.* Paris: F. Lefrançois, 1939.

COURAL, Jean. *Le Palais de l'Élysée. Histoire et décor.* Paris: Délégation à l'action artistique de la Ville de Paris, 1994.

COURAL, Jean, and Guy NICOT. "Le palais de l'Élysée." *Monuments historiques,* no. 132, April–May, 1984, p. 65–88.

DUHAMEL, Patrice and Jacques SANTAMARIA. *L'Élysée. Histoires, secrets, mystères.* New expanded edition. Paris: Plon, 2017.

DULONG, Claude. *La Vie quotidienne à l'Élysée au temps de Charles de Gaulle.* Paris: Hachette, 1974.

DUVAL, Gaston, Henri VIAL, and Charles NORMAND. *Le Palais de l'Élysée, histoire des bâtiments. Notice descriptive des grands appartements.* Paris: Société historique et archéologique du VIIIe arrondissement, April 1903, p. 12.

D'ECOLLES, P. "Le palais de l'Élysée." *Le Monde moderne*, July 1898, p. 95.

FONTAINE, Pierre François Léonard. *Journal, 1799–1853.* Paris: L'École nationale supérieure des beaux-arts/Institut français d'architecture/Société de l'histoire de l'art français, 1987.

GEOFFROY, Pierre and Francesco GUIDOBONI. "Au fil des résidences de Napoléon: de la 'petite maison' au palais de l'Élysée." *ArcHistoR*, no. 13, 2020, p. 107–159.

LEBROUX-CESBRON, Charles. *Le Palais de l'Élysée. Chronique d'un palais national.* Paris: Perrin and Cie, 1925.

MARIETTE, Jean. *L'Architecture française.* Reprint of the original 1727 edition. Vol. III. Paris-Brussels: Van Oest, 1929.

MARMOTTAN, Paul. *Murat à l'Élysée.* Paris: Librairie H. Chéronnet, 1919.

MUTH, Olivier, and Geneviève HAROCHE-BOUZINAC, dir. *Louise de Vilmorin (1902–1969). Une vie à l'œuvre.* Châtenay-Malabry, Maison de Chateaubriand, Ghent: Editions Snoeck, 2019.

OPPERMANN, Fabien. *Dans les châteaux de la République. Le pouvoir à l'abri des regards.* Paris: Tallandier, 2019.

D'ORCIVAL, François. *L'Élysée sous l'Occupation.* Paris: Perrin, 2011.

PASCAL, Camille. *Scènes de la vie quotidienne à l'Élysée. Chroniques.* Paris: Plon, 2012.

PELLISSIER, Pierre. *La Vie quotidienne à l'Élysée au temps de Valéry Giscard d'Estaing.* Paris: Hachette, 1978.

THEILLOU, Françoise. "Malraux décorateur: un salon de musique pour la Lanterne." www.malraux.org, January 2012.

VACQUIER, Jules. *Les Vieux Hôtels de Paris. Le faubourg Saint-Honoré. Décorations extérieures et intérieures.* Vol. II. Paris: F. Contet, 1919.

SOURCES OF QUOTATIONS

DUBUFE, Guillaume. *Rapport sur l'Exposition Universelle de 1900. Rapports du jury international. Classe 7. Peinture, cartons et dessins* (Paris: Imprimerie nationale, 1904).

DE GAULLE, Charles. *Memoirs of Hope: Renewal, 1958–1962,* trans. Terence Kilmartin (London: Weidenfeld & Nicolson, 1971).

GRACQ, Julien. *The Opposing Shore,* trans. Richard Howard (New York: Columbia University Press, 1986).

MALRAUX, André, Minister of Culture, July 31, 1962, from a speech to the National Assembly on the need for a law to protect seven historic monuments (Louvre, Invalides, Versailles, Vincennes, Fontainebleau, Chambord, and Reims Cathedral).

PEYREFITTE, Alain. *C'était de Gaulle* (Paris: Éditions de Fallois-Fayard, 1994).

POMPIDOU, Georges. *Lettres, Notes et Portraits, 1928–1974* (Paris: Livre de Poche, 2014).

STENDHAL. *Lucien Leuwen: The Telegraph,* trans. Louise Varèse (New York: New Directions, 1950).

ACKNOWLEDGMENTS

The publisher, the author, the photographer, and all those who took part in this work express their gratitude to the President of the Republic and his wife. Without their continual goodwill this book would not have been possible. At the Élysée Palace and in the heritage department, Jean Salomon, Director of Resources and Modernization, provided the best support at every stage of this project. Thanks also to Pierre-Olivier Costa, Tristan Bromet, Thomas Christoux, Sylvain Moisy, Marianne Fuseau, Philippe Servent, Marie Talucier, and Evelyne Van Den Neste, as well as Nicolas and Ludivine Tavelet, and Gérald Charton.

At the Mobilier National, Hervé Lemoine was an indispensable contact, as was Thierry Sarmant, Muriel Barbier, Arnaud Denis, Laure Dauvier, Hélène Cavalié, and Fanny Bigeon. At Sèvres – National Manufacture and Museum, Romane Sarfati, Charlotte Vignon, and Sylvie Perrin were invaluable in their assistance.

The author express his warmest thanks to Suzanne Tise-Isoré, Karine Huguenaud, Bernard Lagacé, Lara Lo Calzo, and Virginie Picat of Flammarion, Style & Design Collection.

He owes a lot to those who, over the years, allowed him to discover these places or who gave him good advice: Philippe Bélaval, Louis Benech, Pierre Bonnaure, Emmanuel Bréon, Laurence des Cars, Défendin Détard, Marie-Bénédicte Diethelm, Béatrice de Durfort, Deke Dusinberre, Côme Fabre, Sylvain Fort—who first had the idea for this book—Olivier Gabet, Constance Guisset, Jean-François Hébert, Martin Jahan de Lestang, Alexandre Lafore, Laurent Le Bon, Christophe Leribault, Antonin Macé de Lépinay, Rémi Mathis, Jean-Christophe Mikhaïloff, Fabien Oppermann, Christophe Parant, Camille Pascal, Héléna Perroud, Pauline Prévost-Marcilhacy, François Richier, Alain Seban, and Jean-Michel Wilmotte.

Over the months, the vision of Ambroise Tézenas has been essential; this book could not have existed without his photographer's eye.

INDEX

Page numbers in italic refer to captions.

M

N

O

P

R

S

T

V

W

Z

PHOTOGRAPHIC CREDITS

t: top, b: bottom, l: left, r: right, c: center

All photographs in this book were taken by Ambroize Tézenas except those on the following pages:
pp. 14–15: ©Paris Musées, Musée Carnavalet, Dist. RMN-Grand Palais/image ville de Paris; p. 20: ©Museumslandschaft Hessen Kassel, Gemäldegalerie Alte Meister/Arno Hensmanns; p. 21: ©Reproduction Benjamin Gavaudo/CMN; p. 22: ©AKG-images; p. 24: ©BPK, Berlin, Dist. RMN-Grand Palais/image BStGS; pp. 26–27: ©BnF; p. 28t: ©RMN-Grand Palais/Agence Bulloz; p. 30t: © Lucas Olivet/Genève Enchères ; p. 30l: ©AKG-images; p. 30r: ©RMN-Grand Palais (Louvre Museum)/Jean-Gilles Berizzi; p. 31: ©The National Gallery, London, Dist. RMN-Grand Palais; p. 32: ©Musée Carnavalet/Roger Viollet; p. 33: ©Bridgeman Images ID Photo/Josse; p. 34: ©RMN-Grand Palais (Château de Versailles)/Gérard Blot; pp. 38–39: ©Private collection; p. 40: ©Stefano Bianchetti/Bridgeman; p.41: ©Château de Fontainebleau, Distr. RMN-Grand Palais/Philippe Fuzeau; p. 42t: ©BnF; p. 42b: ©Image ID ©MEPL/Bridgeman Images; p. 43: ©API/Gamma-Rapho/Getty Images; p. 47: ©BnF; p. 48: ©Château de Versailles, Dist. RMN-Grand Palais/image château de Versailles; p. 49t: ©BnF; p. 49b: ©AKG-images; pp. 50–51: ©Stefano Bianchetti/Bridgeman Images; p. 52: ©BnF; p. 53t: ©BnF; p. 53b: ©BnF; p. 54: ©Félix Peaucou/Courtesy of Roland and Axel Tisserand; p. 55: ©BnF; p. 56: ©Archives Nationales Service photographique de la Présidence de la République; p. 57: ©Félix Peaucou/Courtesy of Roland and Axel Tisserand; p. 58t: ©Photo Ingi Paris/AKG-images; p. 58b: ©Claude Azoulay/ParisMatch/Scoop; p. 60: ©AKG-images/Paul Almasy; p. 61: ©René Vital/ParisMatch/Scoop; p. 62t: ©AKG-images/Paul Almasy; p. 62b: ©AKG-images; p. 63t: ©AKG-images/Jacqueline Guillot (CDA); p.63l: ©Photo Ingi Paris/AKG-images; p.63r: ©AKG-images/Paul Almasy; p. 64tl: ©Coll. Bibliothèque municipale de Dijon/MIV1384; p. 64tr: ©Coll. Bibliothèque municipale de Dijon/MIII182; p. 64c: ©Coll. Bibliothèque municipale de Dijon/MIII2309; p. 65t: ©Coll. Bibliothèque municipale de Dijon/MIII823; p. 65c: ©Coll. Bibliothèque municipale de Dijon/MIII2778; p. 65b: ©Coll. Bibliothèque municipale de Dijon/MIII2827; pp. 66–67: ©Photo Ingi Paris/AKG-images; p. 68t: ©The Estate of Jacques Lowe/Premium Archive/Getty Images; p. 68b: ©Reporters Associés/Gamma-Rapho/Getty Images; p. 69 ©Keystones-France/Gamma-Rapho/Getty Images; p. 70t: ©Ministère de la Culture – Médiathèque de l'architecture et du patrimoine, Dist. RMN-Grand Palais/François Kollar; p. 70b: ©Jean Mainbourg/Gamma Rapho/Getty Images; p. 71: ©AKG-images; pp. 72–73: ©Keystones-France/Gamma-Rapho/Getty Images; p. 76: ©Centre Pompidou, MNAM-CCI Dist. RMN-Grand Palais/Jacqueline Hyde; p. 77: ©Keystone/Hulton Archives (Getty Images); p. 78: ©Centre Pompidou MNAM-C€I, Dist. RMN-Grand Palais/Georges Meguerditchian; p. 79: ©AKG-images/CDA/Guillemot; p. 82: ©Jean-Régis Roustan/Roger-Viollet; p. 83: ©Dominique Berretty/Gamma-Rapho/Getty Images; pp. 84–85: ©Georges Fessy/Artedia/Bridgeman Images; p. 86: ©Musées de la Ville de Boulogne-Billancourt ; p. 87t: ©Mobilier National/Philippe Sébert; p. 87b: © Musées de la Ville de Boulogne-Billancourt/cortesy of Pierre-Christophe Baguet, Maire de Boulogne-Billancourt, Président de Grand Paris Seine Ouest; p. 88:©Philippe Petit/ParisMatch/Scoop; p. 89t: ©Manuel Cohen/Aurimages; p. 89b: ©Mobilier National/All rights reserved pp. 90–91: ©David Giancatarina/Sèvres-Manufacture et Musée Nationaux; p.93: ©Jean-Pierre Couderc/Roger Viollet; p. 96: ©Arnaud Roiné/Divergence Images; p. 97: ©Arnaud Roiné/Divergence Images; p. 102t: ©RMN-Grand Palais (Château de Versailles)/Gérard Blot; p. 102b: ©Jacques Cuinières/Roger-Viollet; p. 103r: ©IMEC; Fonds MCC, Dist. RMN-Grand Palais/Gisèle Freund; p. 103l: ©IMEC, Fonds MCC, Dist. RMN-Grand Palais/Gisèle Freund; p. 103r: ©Soazig de la Moissonnière/Présidence de la République ; p. 104: ©Musée Carnavalet/Roger Viollet; p. 110: ©Alexandre Serebriakoff/Adagp, Paris, 2021/AKG-Images/De Agostini Picture Lib./G. Dagli Orti; p. 111: ©Alexandre Serebriakoff/Adagp, Paris, 2021/AKG-images; pp. 150-51: ©Olivier Amsellem; p. 153l: ©AKG–images/CDA/Guillemot; p. 153r: © Olivier Amsellem; p. 243: ©RMN-Grand Palais (Château de Versailles)/Gérard Blot; p. 244: ©IMEC, Fonds MCC, Dist. RMN-Grand Palais/Gisèle Freund; p. 245: ©Mobilier National/Isabelle Bideau; p. 276: ©BnF; p. 279t: ©François Page/ParisMatch/Scoop; p. 279b: ©Félix Golesi/Bestimage; pp. 280–81: ©Picture Alliance/Getty Images.

COPYRIGHT INFORMATION